Negotiating from Strength

Leverage in U.S.-Soviet Arms Control Negotiations

THE WASHINGTON PAPERS

. . . intended to meet the need for an authoritative, yet prompt, public appraisal of the major developments in world affairs.

Series Editors: Walter Laqueur; Amos A. Jordan

Associate Editors: William J. Taylor, Jr.; M. Jon Vondracek

Executive Editor: Jean C. Newsom

Managing Editor: Nancy B. Eddy

MANUSCRIPT SUBMISSION

The Washington Papers and Praeger Publishers welcome inquiries concerning manuscript submissions. Please include with your inquiry a curriculum vita, synopsis, table of contents, and estimated manuscript length. Submissions to *The Washington Papers* should be sent to *The Washington Papers*; The Center for Strategic and International Studies; Georgetown University; 1800 K Street NW; Suite 400; Washington, DC 20006. Book proposals should be sent to Praeger Publishers; 521 Fifth Avenue; New York NY 10175.

Negotiating from Strength

Leverage in U.S.-Soviet Arms Control Negotiations

Robert J. Einhorn

Foreword by William G. Hyland

Published with The Center for
Strategic and International Studies,
Georgetown University, Washington, D.C.

PRAEGER SPECIAL STUDIES • PRAEGER SCIENTIFIC

Library of Congress Cataloging in Publication Data

Einhorn, Robert J.
   Negotiating from strength.

   (The Washington papers, ISSN 0278-937X ;
vol. XIII, 113)
   1. Nuclear arms control – United States.
2. Nuclear arms control – Soviet Union.   I. Title.
II. Series.
JX1974.7.E38   1985   327.1'74   85-3409
ISBN 0-03-005534-2
ISBN 0-03-004769-2 (pbk)

Published in 1985 by Praeger Publishers
CBS Educational and Professional Publishing, a Division of CBS Inc.
521 Fifth Avenue, New York, NY 10175 USA

© 1985 by The Center for Strategic and International Studies

Printed in the United States of America on acid-free paper

INTERNATIONAL OFFICES

Orders from outside the United States should be sent to the appropriate address listed below. Orders from
areas not listed below should be placed through CBS International Publishing, 383 Madison Ave., New York,
NY 10175 USA

Australia, New Zealand
Holt Saunders, Pty, Ltd., 9 Waltham St., Artarmon, N.S.W. 2064, Sydney, Australia
Canada
Holt, Rinehart & Winston of Canada, 55 Horner Ave., Toronto, Ontario, Canada M8Z 4X6
Europe, the Middle East, & Africa
Holt Saunders, Ltd., 1 St. Anne's Road, Eastbourne, East Sussex, England BN21 3UN
Japan
Holt Saunders, Ltd., Ichibancho Central Building, 22-1 Ichibancho, 3rd Floor, Chiyodaku, Tokyo, Japan
Hong Kong, Southeast Asia
Holt Saunders Asia, Ltd., 10 Fl, Intercontinental Plaza, 94 Granville Road, Tsim Sha Tsui East, Kowloon,
Hong Kong

Manuscript submissions should be sent to the Editorial Director, Praeger Publishers, 521 Fifth Avenue, New
York, NY 10175 USA

Published and Distributed by the
   Praeger Publishers Division
   (ISBN Prefix 0-275)
   of Greenwood Press, Inc.,
   Westport, Connecticut

Contents

Foreword

For the past 40 years the United States and the Soviet Union have been engaged in negotiations about the limitation of arms. Since 1969, with the beginning of the strategic arms limitations talks, these negotiations have been increasingly intensive – and, of course, controversial. Not only has the outcome of the various negotiations been subject to scrutiny, but the negotiating process itself has come to interest scholars and political leaders, as well as the negotiators themselves. A body of theory has gradually been developed that suggests certain conclusions. The current study by Robert Einhorn belongs in this category of new studies and is an outstanding piece of analysis.

The study of negotiating techniques is not new. Gaining leverage over an adversary is the oldest of objectives. Compromise and bargaining are relatively easy concepts to understand. But nuclear arms have given these standard terms a new significance. In particular, the relationship between the objects of the negotiations – arms – and the outcome of the negotiations – agreements – has taken on a new meaning. That aspect is summed up in the phrase "bargaining chips." In other words, the weapons themselves have an existence beyond their military utility or desirability. They have a value within the negotiations: they are tradable. This, in turn, has led to another phenomenon, the justification of weapons—not to counter an opponent's weapons on the battlefield, but to counter them at the negotiating table. This has transformed the entire planning of defense, both in the development and procurement of weapons. Programs are no longer presented, rationalized, or justified primarily by strategy or budgetary considerations. They are inevitably related to current or forthcoming negotiations. Almost every recent U.S. strategic program has undergone this new process, beginning in the late 1960s with the antiballistic missile, the first and most famous (or infamous) of the bargaining chips. Many systems such as the cruise missile and the MX have been sustained by the arms control-bargaining chip argument.

In this connection, another related phenomenon is the transformation of what begins as bargaining chips into solid assets not to be traded at any price. The U.S. cruise missile is the prime example. Saved from the Pentagon axe in the early 1970s by Henry Kissinger, it gradually became a critical program. Within a few years the idea of limiting or banning cruise missiles was regarded as a major concession to the Soviets. Within a few more years, the land-based cruise missile in Europe had become completely transformed to the point that its deployment was an overriding U.S. and NATO objective. This interplay has obviously led to second thoughts about creating weapons as bargaining chips.

The two sides, U.S. and Soviet, have approached this process quite differently, in part because their approach to negotiations as a whole is markedly different. The Americans are prone to look for the end result and gear their proposals to accomplish an outcome. Thus "trade-offs" are always under consideration. The Soviets are much less interested in this approach. They concentrate on preserving what they consider essential from a strategic or military viewpoint. Hence they are loathe to consider compromises in which they trade their systems against a U.S. system, whether the system is comparable or not. They are very interested, however, in trading what does not exist against some U.S. program that is still in research. This has become the classic confrontation over the U.S. Strategic Defense Initiative.

All of these aspects are treated in detail together with shrewd appraisals in Mr. Einhorn's study. As both a student of the process and a practitioner, he is able to bring unusual insights to bear. The result is a significant work, especially to be pondered as the laborious arms control process begins anew in Geneva. Both sides undoubtedly harbor the aim of entering these new talks from a position of strength. What this means in practice and the consequences that flow from this understandable ambition are the subject of the pages that follow, which now invite the reader's attention.

William G. Hyland
Editor, *Foreign Affairs*
February 1985

About the Author

Robert Einhorn is currently a member of the U.S. Delegation to the Strategic Arms Reduction Talks with the Soviet Union. He wrote this volume while on leave from the U.S. government as an international affairs fellow of the Council on Foreign Relations. During his fellowship year he was also a visiting scholar at Georgetown University's Center for Strategic and International Studies, where he served as executive director of the Center's group on Strategy and Arms Control. Since 1972 Einhorn has held a variety of positions at the U.S. Arms Control and Disarmament Agency, where he has been involved in negotiations on nuclear weapons testing, strategic arms, chemical weapons, and nuclear nonproliferation. In 1982 and 1983 he was a member of the U.S. Delegation to the Strategic Arms Reductions Talks in Geneva. The views expressed in this volume do not necessarily represent those of the U.S. government.

Negotiating from Strength

Leverage in U.S.-Soviet
Arms Control Negotiations

1

The Debate on Negotiating Leverage

The combination of the Reagan administration's ambitious arms control proposals and its ambitious weapon modernization plans—especially plans for such controversial systems as the missile experimental (MX), binary chemical munitions, and antisatellite (ASAT) weapons—has rekindled one of the longest-standing disputes in arms control—the debate over the impact of U.S. weapon programs on prospects for success in arms control negotiations with the Soviet Union.

Roughly speaking, the debate can be divided into two camps. The first, which has tended to dominate official Washington thinking throughout most of the postwar era of arms control, has maintained that active U.S. defense programs provide essential bargaining leverage—specifically, that such programs increase the prospects for Soviet negotiating concessions and, eventually, for agreements acceptable to the United States.

According to this view, U.S. weapon systems, deployed or under development, can influence the behavior of the Soviets at the negotiating table by altering their calculations of risk and benefit, bringing them to the conclusion that they would be better off accepting mutual limitations than allowing the military programs of both sides to continue unconstrained. The opportunity to limit those U.S. systems is what motivates the Soviets to consider constraints on themselves. Without those systems as bargaining assets, so the argument goes, the likelihood of obtaining limits on Soviet capabilities would be virtually nil.

The opposing side in the debate argues that U.S. weapon programs, instead of encouraging receptivity to mutual limits, have tended to strengthen Soviet determination to initiate or accelerate programs designed to offset U.S. advances and prevent the USSR from falling behind. The net effect, these critics say, is to stimulate a new competition in arms, to delay or even to foreclose the possibility of negotiated limits, and often to weaken the security of both sides. They maintain that new programs, rather than serving as trading capital, tend to acquire strong supporters within the bureaucracy and the Congress who strenuously resist efforts to limit them, or even include them, in negotiations.

Proponents of the first view point to a variety of cases in which U.S. programs appeared to play a critical role in promoting Soviet acceptance of mutual limitations. The example invariably cited in this connection is the Anti-Ballistic Missile (ABM) Treaty, in which the initiation of a U.S. ABM program seems to have been largely responsible for an abrupt turnaround in Soviet attitudes toward ABM restraints.

At the Glassboro summit in June 1967, Soviet Premier Alexei N. Kosygin brushed aside U.S. efforts to discuss limits on defensive systems. But after congressional support for the Johnson administration's Sentinel ABM program in 1968 and (by one Senate vote) for Phase I of the Nixon administration's renamed Safeguard ABM program in 1969, the Soviets apparently took a major policy decision to pursue restrictive limits on ABM deployments in the Strategic Arms Limitation Talks (SALT) I negotiations. Their primary motive was presumably the calculation, based in part on the disappointing performance of their first generation ABM system, that they would finish a distant second in any all-out ABM competition — and indeed that a successful U.S. program might eventually jeopardize the retaliatory capability and overall strategic position they had been working so hard to achieve. The result was the ABM Treaty of 1972.[1]

A second example is the SALT II Treaty. At the risk of grossly oversimplifying a complex agreement, it seems that the essential SALT II trade-off involved modest constraints on Soviet intercontinental ballistic missile (ICBM) capabilities in exchange for modest constraints on U.S. cruise missile capabilities. U.S. concerns were addressed, but by no means eliminated, by such provisions as the sublimit of 820 ICBMs carrying multiple independently targetable reentry vehicles (MIRVs), the limit of 10 warheads per ICBM, the reduction in delivery vehicles to 2,250 (forcing the retirement of some older ICBMs), and the ceilings on the permissible weights of "light" and "heavy" ICBMS. Although these constraints did not preclude extensive Soviet ICBM modernization programs, they probably stopped those programs short of planned levels and bounded the Soviet ICBM threat predictably enough to permit the design of a multiple-shelter basing arrangement aimed at making the MX adequately survivable against Soviet attack.[2]

Soviet concerns were addressed, although hardly more satisfactorily than were U.S. concerns, by such provisions as the inclusion of heavy bombers equipped for air-launched cruise missiles (ALCMs) in the 1,320 aggregate for multiple-weapon delivery vehicles, the ban on deploying long-range ALCMs on aircraft other than heavy bombers (thus prohibiting them on U.S. shorter-range aircraft forward based in Europe and Asia), ceilings on the numbers of ALCMs carried on heavy bombers, and a ban on the deployment (but not the testing or production) of long-range ground-launched (GLCMs) and sea-launched (SLCMs) cruise missiles during a protocol period lasting only through 1981. Although these constraints permitted a large U.S. ALCM deployment, enabled U.S. development and testing of SLCMs and GLCMs to proceed on schedule, and did not preclude SLCM and GLCM deployment after expiration of the brief protocol, they nonetheless put a cap on the U.S. ALCM threat and gave the Soviets an opportunity at a later date to try to extend the protocol's restrictions on SLCM and GLCM deployment or make them permanent.

In a negotiation like SALT involving numerous weapon systems, trade-offs, and package proposals, it is often difficult to sort out why key concessions were made and in exchange precisely for what. But the evidence suggests that constraints on ICBM capabilities, as modest as they were, were facilitated by – and probably would not have been negotiable without – U.S. willingness to accept the limits that were placed on its cruise missile programs. This conclusion is supported by the key trade-off reached in September 1977, in which Soviet Foreign Minister Andrei Gromyko agreed for the first time (after several previous U.S. attempts) to limit MIRVed ICBMs, but only on the condition that heavy bombers equipped for ALCMs be included in the aggregate for multiple-weapon delivery vehicles.

A third case in which U.S. programs have led to more flexible Soviet negotiating behavior is in the area of intermediate-range nuclear forces (INF). Discussions in the North Atlantic Treaty Organization (NATO) in 1978 and 1979 on a Western response to Soviet SS-20 deployments seem to have prompted a turnabout in Moscow's previous reluctance to discuss limits on Soviet INF systems. In October 1979, in an effort to head off NATO's impending decision to deploy 572 U.S. GLCMs and Pershing II missiles in Western Europe, Soviet leader Leonid I. Brezhnev offered to reduce the level of Soviet medium-range systems in Europe and to enter into negotiations on such systems, provided that no NATO missiles were deployed. After NATO went ahead with its decision in December 1979 to deploy new INF missiles in the absence of an arms control agreement making such deployment unnecessary, the Soviets first retracted the offer to negotiate, but then agreed in the summer of 1980 to enter into talks when it became clear that their efforts to sidetrack the NATO decision in the absence of negotiations were not succeeding.

In the course of those negotiations, the Soviets demonstrated, through a succession of proposals, that they were prepared to pay a significant price to prevent the NATO deployment. The final offer they made before walking out of the talks in November 1983 was their "equal reductions" proposal. Under that proposal, they would dismantle 572 warheads on INF missiles in the western USSR (all remaining SS-4s and well over 100 modern SS-20s) as well as freeze deployment in the eastern USSR – but with the proviso that the United States agree to abandon its deployment program altogether, a condition considered unacceptable by NATO. Thus, although the INF modernization program has not produced enough Soviet flexibility to meet NATO's requirements for an agreement, it has already led to concessions that, by Soviet standards, are impressive – that is, dismantling of modern, newly deployed systems in exchange for the nondeployment of yet-to-be deployed systems.

A fourth example of bargaining leverage provided by U.S. programs involves ASAT. As the United States has progressed in the development of its F-15-based ASAT system, the Soviet Union's interest in ASAT limitations has intensified and its willingness to limit its own programs has increased.

In the bilateral talks held in 1978 and 1979, the Soviets were unreceptive to the U.S. proposal for a comprehensive ASAT prohibition and instead favored a ban on the use, but not the possession, of such systems. In 1981, with the bilateral talks suspended in the wake of the 1979 Soviet invasion of Afghanistan and the advent of a new U.S. administration in Washington, the Soviets tabled a draft treaty at the United Nations that would ban the stationing of weapons in space and outlaw certain hostile acts against space vehicles, but would not affect earth-based ASAT weapons such as their existing system.

Then in August 1983, with initial flight-testing of the U.S. ASAT system rapidly approaching, General Secretary Yuri V. Andropov announced that the USSR would observe a moratorium on launches of ASAT weapons into space as long as the United States practiced similar restraint. And, going beyond the 1981 draft treaty, he proposed an agreement that would eliminate existing ASAT systems and ban the development of new ones. Although current prospects for meaningful ASAT negotiations are uncertain, it seems clear that movement in the Soviet position, especially the recent willingness to dismantle existing Soviet interceptor systems, can be attributed to Soviet concerns about the impending U.S. ASAT capability.

Those who are skeptical of the utility of U.S. weapon programs as negotiating tools focus on other examples from the historical record. For them, the "classic" case is MIRV. They point out that, despite a several-year lead in MIRV technology and calls for self-restraint by congressional opponents of MIRV, the United States began the flight-testing of MIRVed systems for Minuteman III and Poseidon in the summer of 1968 and eventually completed the test programs during the early stages of SALT I. A brief, and some say perfunctory, U.S. effort was made to ban MIRV in 1970, but was abandoned when the Soviets responded with a counterproposal unacceptable to the United States.[3] Thus, despite claims advanced at the time that MIRV would provide the United States substantial negotiating leverage, the U.S. MIRV program neither resulted in constraints on Soviet MIRVs nor was used to obtain limits on other Soviet programs. Instead, it stimulated Soviet MIRVing efforts, which eventually resulted in the vulnerability of U.S. land-based forces.

Cruise missiles are also frequently mentioned as failed bargaining chips. Although cruise missiles helped achieve some modest limits on ICBM capabilities in SALT II, critics point out that the SALT II Treaty permits very large numbers of ALCMs, that the protocol's expiration leaves SLCMs and GLCMs unconstrained, and that certain features of cruise missiles such as dual (conventional-nuclear) capability and common airframes will plague future attempts at arms control, especially now that missiles of all three basing modes have been tested extensively and deployed. Moreover, they argue that the intensification of the U.S. interest in cruise missiles in the early 1970s stimulated Soviet long-range ALCM, GLCM, and SLCM programs, which, although still technically inferior to their U.S. counterparts, are expected eventually to pose serious threats to the United States and its allies. The irony, the critics say, is that former Secretary of State Henry A. Kissinger's desire for increased bargaining leverage in SALT II gave a high-level push to cruise missile programs that might not otherwise have made their way up from the depths of the service bureaucracies.

A few examples have also been cited in which, contrary to conventional bargaining-chip wisdom, the United States obtained limits on Soviet military capabilities without having active military programs of its own to put forward as negotiating capital. In 1974, for example, the Soviets agreed in the protocol to the ABM Treaty to reduce the number of permitted ABM complexes from two to one, even though Congress had already turned down funds for an ABM complex to defend Washington D.C. and it was clear that the United States would not be able to exercise its right to construct a second site. Similarly, the Soviets in 1972 signed the Biological Weapons (BW) Convention obligating them to destroy their existing stocks of such weapons despite the fact that three years earlier the United States had decided unilaterally to renounce BWs and get rid of its own supply. Neither action can be explained strictly in terms of a Soviet interest in a military quid pro quo.

Moreover, those who question the correlation between U.S. defense programs and negotiating success point out that, even though the Reagan administration managed to get virtually its entire strategic modernization program through Congress, the Soviets did not respond with the flexibility that some officials had expected and instead suspended the Strategic Arms Reduction Talks (START) indefinitely in December 1983 on the grounds that U.S. deployment of INF missiles in Europe required a review of the Soviet approach to strategic arms negotiations.

As demonstrated by these examples, the historical record so frequently invoked by both sides in the debate is, in fact, rather mixed. Sometimes U.S. defense programs are instrumental in obtaining Soviet concessions; sometimes they are not. What the record shows is that the issue of negotiating leverage is more complicated than categorical assertions either that U.S. programs promote arms control agreements or that such programs stimulate arms races.

On the one hand, the record suggests that it is unrealistic to expect the Soviets to accept significant limitations on their military capabilities if we do not have programs that we are prepared to limit in return. The Soviets, as most observers of their negotiating behavior point out, do not believe in charity — especially in matters of national security. They will not give up something without receiving compensating benefits. And in most cases — and in all cases where they give up something of substantial military importance — those benefits will include limits on U.S. military capabilities.[4]

Thus, U.S. programs are usually a necessary condition for inducing the Soviets to accept limits on their own military capabilities. Without such programs, it is unlikely that there would be an ABM Treaty, that the Soviets would have agreed to even the modest ICBM constraints of SALT II, or that they would have made significant concessions (or perhaps even engaged) in the ASAT and INF negotiations.

On the other hand, the record also indicates that it is unrealistic to expect that simply acquiring an impressive array of weapon systems will somehow lead automatically to the achievement of U.S. negotiating objectives. Although U.S. programs can be necessary ingredients in the bargaining process, they are often not sufficient to produce success, or even progress, in the negotiations. For several reasons, U.S. ability to influence Soviet negotiating behavior by pursuing defense programs is both far more limited and far less calculable than advocates of "negotiating from strength" care to admit.

First, just because "strength" (in the form of defense programs) will usually be a prerequisite for successful bargaining does not mean that all U.S. programs provide equally effective leverage. Although certain programs may pose a serious challenge to the Soviets and create powerful incentives for them to make concessions, others may cause only marginal

concern in the Kremlin and provide little stimulus for negotiations. Some may cause concern but prompt the Soviets to
alleviate that concern through their own defense efforts rather than arms control. Still other programs may provide potential leverage, but the United States may decide, for various
reasons, to keep them out of the bargaining process and thus
not exploit that potential.

Second, although U.S. programs can provide incentives
for the Soviets to accept mutual limitations, the United States
is certainly not in a position—given the impressive size and
momentum of Soviet military programs and the apparent
Soviet determination to allocate to defense whatever scarce
resources are deemed necessary—to call the tune in arms control negotiations. The Soviets will accept agreements only
if they calculate that they would be better off, or at least no
worse off, than they would be in the absence of mutual constraints. In making such calculations, the Soviets normally
place a higher priority on protecting their own capabilities
than limiting ours, and, in particular, they give considerable
weight to preserving capabilities such as powerful, accurate
ICBMs that they consider essential to their strategic objectives. So even when defense programs give the United States
negotiating leverage, they may not give us enough to obtain
the particular limits we seek on Soviet forces. Indeed, certain constraints on Soviet capabilities may simply not be
negotiable, at least not at any price the United States would
conceivably be able and willing to pay.

Third, military factors are not the only ones influencing
Soviet negotiating behavior. Naturally, the Soviets will carefully analyze the military implications of any proposed arms
control arrangement, and such analysis will have a major impact on Soviet decision making. But a wide range of nonmilitary considerations, including foreign policy objectives, domestic incentives and disincentives, and economic influences,
can also play an important role in moving the Soviets toward
or away from accommodation in arms control. In some cases,
these considerations will provide the principal Soviet motivation for agreement. In almost all cases, they will affect the

timing of negotiations—and indeed whether an agreement can be concluded at all. And, despite the importance of these nonmilitary factors in Soviet negotiating behavior, the United States will often be unaware of their existence—and unable to influence them even when it is.

Thus, to have realistic expectations about the negotiating process, it is necessary to recognize not only the importance (and often the indispensability) of active U.S. weapon programs, but also the substantial limitations and uncertainties involved in seeking to use those programs to influence Soviet behavior. Unfortunately, in highly polarized defense funding battles, one or the other of these considerations tends to get ignored by advocates of opposing sides. Arguments about the utility of bargaining chips—pro and con—are tossed around almost casually and seem to be based not on any informed analysis of likely Soviet attitudes and reactions toward the particular programs in question, but on clichés and biases that vary little from case to dissimilar case.

What makes matters worse is that arguments about the presumed diplomatic value of defense programs have begun to play an inordinately powerful role in the weapon acquisition process. Discussion of how, for example, the MX and binary chemical weapons would affect deterrence and fit into the overall U.S. military posture tend to get submerged by vague assertions about whether the U.S. negotiator will be strengthened or undermined, whether right or wrong signals will be sent, and so forth. With the public's heightened interest in arms control, this trend may be difficult to reverse. But as long as assessments of the negotiating value of defense programs are going to affect the procurement process, it is important at least that those assessments be made as accurate as possible.

Without a better understanding of how, and the extent to which, U.S. programs influence Soviet arms control behavior, there is a risk of distorting U.S. force planning, because programs may be approved or disapproved on the basis of misconceptions about their utility as negotiating tools. There is also a risk of jeopardizing prospects for worthwhile arms control—either by underestimating U.S. negotiating leverage and thereby missing opportunities, or by overestimating U.S. leverage and consequently setting unrealistic negotiating objectives.

Of course, U.S. understanding of how, and the extent to which, it can influence Soviet negotiating behavior—whether through defense programs or through other means—will necessarily remain quite limited. Given the opaque character of the Soviet system, U.S. knowledge of what motivates Soviet decisions will always be, to say the least, imperfect. But even if the United States can never measure negotiating incentives with precision or predict Soviet negotiating behavior with confidence, perhaps it can gain a better understanding than it currently has of factors that determine the utility—and limitations—of U.S. defense programs as negotiating tools. In seeking such a better understanding, we should look at three factors that help shape Soviet negotiating behavior:

- the extent to which various U.S. defense programs provide incentives for the Soviets to accept limits on their programs;
- the degree to which the Soviets value different programs of their own and are prepared to restrict them in exchange for limits on U.S. capabilities;
- the role of nonmilitary considerations in providing incentives or disincentives for movement toward arms control agreements.

These three factors are explored in chapters 2, 3, and 4, respectively. Chapter 5, drawing on the analysis in the preceding chapters, discusses some current controversies regarding negotiating leverage. Finally, chapter 6 provides some concluding observations on the impact of U.S. weapon programs on Soviet negotiating behavior.

2

U.S. Programs and Their Impact on Soviet Negotiating Incentives

U.S. negotiating leverage is, in part, a function of Soviet interest in imposing arms control limitations on U.S. defense programs. The stronger the Soviet interest in obtaining limits on U.S. programs, the greater will be their incentive to accept limits on Soviet capabilities in exchange for restrictions on those programs.

But arms control is obviously not the only option available to the Soviets for alleviating their concerns about U.S. defense programs. In fact, it is rarely the most important option. The Soviets depend primarily on their own unilateral defense efforts to match or otherwise offset the effects of U.S. military programs. Often Soviet defense efforts are already underway before the advent of corresponding U.S. programs, in which case the Soviet response may involve accelerating or increasing the scale of an ongoing program rather than initiating one that would otherwise not be pursued.

In a substantial number of cases, the Soviets adopt a two-pronged approach to avoid or minimize the adverse effects of U.S. military developments. One prong involves seeking to constrain U.S. programs—preferably by using propaganda and other political techniques to encourage unilateral U.S. restraint, but, if that is not promising, by promoting mutual arms control limitations. The other prong involves proceeding concurrently and energetically with whatever military action they deem necessary to counter those U.S. programs should their attempts to constrain them fail. This is essentially the two-pronged approach the Soviets have taken over the last decade in response to heightened U.S. interest in long-range cruise missiles in the mid-1970s. But although the Soviets may at times give considerable emphasis to arms control in such a strategy, they rarely, if ever, rely exclusively on arms control to solve their security concerns without having defense programs in train as a hedge against the inability to achieve their objectives through negotiations (or through political campaigns to encourage U.S. self-restraint).

Thus, the Soviets have the option to compete rather than accommodate, and the availability of that option clearly places limits on U.S. ability to influence their negotiating behavior through defense programs. The availability of the option to compete does not mean the Soviets will always see an advantage in competing, however. Indeed, they will calculate that, in certain areas of defense, the costs of competition would be high and the probable rewards low, and they will therefore determine that their interests would best be served by negotiating mutual limitations.

In considering when they should give greater emphasis to arms control and when they could afford to compete, the Soviets have followed a consistent pattern based on the comparative military advantages of the two sides—the traditional U.S. advantage in technological innovation and the traditional Soviet advantage in numbers. Accordingly, they have often sought to use arms control as a means of banning new military developments, thereby blocking off entire channels of future competition perceived to be unfavorable to them. It is in this area of constraining new weapon developments that the Soviet Union has typically been the initiator of arms control proposals, the demandeur, and where they have had the strongest incentives to come to terms with the United States.

The Soviet attitude toward restricting the size of U.S.

programs has normally been much more relaxed. The Soviets have been interested in avoiding numerical imbalances unfavorable to them, just as they have sought to prevent U.S. qualitative advantages. But the quantitative threat posed by the United States has been much less worrisome to them, given their own ability to turn out weapons in large numbers. Thus, although the Soviets have been prepared to accept limitations or even reductions in existing military capabilities, they have not been under great pressure to do so, certainly not on terms they considered disadvantageous. Indeed, the United States has usually been the demandeur for constraints on existing military forces.

This chapter discusses Soviet attitudes toward constraining U.S. defense programs and the extent to which those programs are a source of negotiating leverage in arms control. It first looks at Soviet interest in prohibiting new weapon developments, explaining why the Soviets assign a higher priority to outlawing some U.S. programs than others and describing how their approach toward constraining particular programs will often change when their proposal to ban the programs does not prove negotiable. It then looks at Soviet attitudes toward restricting rather than banning systems, exploring why the United States has had difficulty in the last 15 years of arms control negotiations in trying to slow and reverse Soviet quantitative momentum in weapon categories of particular concern.

Incentives to Ban
New U.S. Weapon Developments

Naturally, if the Soviets could have all their arms control wishes granted, they would wish to have all new U.S. defense programs banned. But they know that, realistically, this would require them to pay an exorbitant price in limits on their own capabilities. And so, as the historical record makes clear, they establish priorities, distinguishing between new

U.S. programs they strongly hope to stop and those they are better prepared to live with and compete against.

High Priority Items

In general, the Soviets have been most concerned about U.S. programs they believe will pose a qualitatively new and challenging threat. In most cases, such programs fall in the area of advanced technology. Part of their preoccupation with U.S. high technology programs stems from their respect for U.S. technological prowess and their apprehension that such programs could give the United States a substantial – even if sometimes only temporary – military advantage. The Soviets probably believe that, unlike the incremental gains that might be obtained from, say, a generational improvement in ICBMs, the advantages that might accrue from a breakthrough in, for example, exotic ballistic missile defense technologies could have a major, if not decisive, impact on the strategic balance.

Quite apart from their worry about possible U.S. advantages, the Soviets wish to restrict technological advances because their rigid system of long-range planning cannot adapt easily to a rapidly changing threat. They place a high premium on predictability, on being able to assess the future threat confidently and accurately and to plan against it well in advance. U.S. programs at the frontiers of technology can undermine that predictability. They can also require a major and sometimes open-ended commitment of Soviet resources to cope with an impending new U.S. capability, which not only can disrupt long-range planning and the delicate balance of bureaucratic forces on which it is often based, but can also place heavy strains on the Soviet economy.

These motivations contributed to the high priority the Soviets gave to banning a U.S. nationwide ABM capability, prohibiting cruise missiles, and blocking the deployment of U.S. intermediate-range missiles in Europe. On the ABM, in addition to foreseeing a widening qualitative gap between their own disappointing Galosh ABM program and its U.S. counterpart, Soviet planners were aware that an effective U.S. ABM system would require major Soviet efforts in offensive forces—on a scale and of a nature hard to predict—to ensure the continued effectiveness of Soviet retaliatory capabilities.

Long-range cruise missiles have troubled the Soviets for several reasons. They require sophisticated guidance, propulsion, electronics, and other technologies in which the United States might be expected to have an edge. With their low-altitude flight and small radar cross section, as well as their ability to be deployed in large numbers (because of their relatively low cost and small size), cruise missiles can substantially reduce the effectiveness of Soviet air defenses and force those defenses to be upgraded at considerable cost. The Soviets have probably calculated that, with the forward-basing opportunities available within the U.S. alliance system, cruise missiles at ranges of 2,000–3,000 kilometers (i.e., the range of current U.S. cruise missiles) could vastly increase the ability of the United States to strike the Soviet homeland with nuclear weapons without providing an equivalent Soviet capability against U.S. territory.[5]

The intensity of Soviet concerns about long-range cruise missile programs can be seen in the persistence with which Soviet negotiators have sought to constrain them. For example, the Soviets rejected the 1976 U.S. proposal to conclude the SALT II agreement as negotiated thus far and to set aside the questions of cruise missiles and the Soviet Backfire bomber for subsequent negotiations. Thus, they turned down an otherwise acceptable SALT agreement (with Backfire, as they insisted, not counted) and accepted the uncertainties associated with a U.S. presidential election and a possible new administration rather than allow U.S. cruise missiles to remain unconstrained.[6]

In the last several years, no U.S. program has generated as much Soviet opposition as has the plan to deploy intermediate-range nuclear forces in Western Europe. Because

NATO's planned INF deployment of 572 missiles consists largely of GLCMs, there is considerable overlap between Soviet concerns about the qualitatively new threat posed by U.S. cruise missiles and their concerns about the current INF program. But cruise missiles deployed on land in Europe raise some distinct and additional problems for the Soviets. One is that GLCMs deployed in Germany could increase the likelihood that any conventional conflict in Central Europe could escalate rapidly to nuclear strikes against the USSR. Another problem is emotional in character for the Soviets – Germany would be the source of such strikes. Third, the Soviets might be concerned that conventionally-armed variants of long-range GLCMs could in the future help NATO out of its long-standing nuclear dilemma.

But Soviet concerns about the INF deployments are clearly not confined to GLCMs. The minimal warning time provided by the Pershing II ballistic missile puts Soviet early warning systems under greater stress than they faced previously.[7] Although the Soviets have gotten some propaganda mileage by exaggerating the Pershing II's ability to reach Moscow, they recognize that, even if the Pershings do not now have sufficient range, they could in the future be upgraded both in range and number (from the currently planned 108) and could then pose a serious threat to Soviet command and control facilities and other time-urgent targets in the western USSR.

The desire to avoid technological surprise and U.S. qualitative advantages has also been reflected in Soviet proposals to curb nuclear weapon testing, antisatellite weapons, and antisubmarine warfare capabilities. The intensity of Soviet concerns varies considerably in these cases with Soviet perceptions of the immediacy and magnitude of the technological threat. Thus, with the United States now proceeding to flight test its F-15 ASAT system, ASAT limitations have become a matter of greater urgency than constraints either on ASW or nuclear weapon testing, where strategically important breakthroughs do not appear imminent. Nonetheless, the nature of Soviet concern is essentially the same.

U.S. Programs of Lower Priority

It is noteworthy that the Soviets have attached considerably less importance to heading off U.S. hard-target counterforce capabilities (i.e., the ability to destroy fixed targets fortified against nuclear blast, such as ICBM silos and command and control bunkers) than to stopping advanced technological developments.[8] This difference in priorities has been reflected in Soviet arms control positions. For example, although Soviet negotiators have been persistent in seeking severe limits on cruise missiles, their efforts to ban such hard-target-capable systems as the MX ICBM and the D-5 SLBM have been half hearted.

In SALT II, the Soviets sought to ban new types of MIRVed ICBMs (including the MX) and to permit one new type of single-warhead ICBM. When the United States resisted, they agreed rather quickly to permit one new type of ICBM, whether MIRVed or single-warhead, thus permitting the MX. Earlier in the SALT II negotiations, the Soviets rejected the U.S. package proposal of March 1977, which would have banned any further ICBM modernization, including the MX program, and would have required the Soviets to reduce their heavy ICBMs from 308 to 150 and to limit their MIRVed ICBMs to 550. Although the Soviets would thus have had to pay a substantial price, they could have prevented the United States from achieving any ICBM hard-target-kill capability and thereby retained a monopoly in that strategic capability.[9] Moreover, the original Soviet START proposal would have prohibited the D-5, the first SLBM with a combination of accuracy and explosive yield sufficient to destroy hardened targets. But one of the first Soviet concessions in START was to drop the proposal.

Considering that the Soviets currently have a much higher share of their strategic assets located at fixed, potentially vulnerable sites than we do, why have they taken a relatively relaxed attitude toward U.S. acquisition of hard-target-capable ballistic missiles? There seem to be several reasons.

First, in their attitude toward the concept of crisis stability, the Soviets apparently attach much less significance than does the United States to the vulnerability of a portion of one's own retaliatory forces. They probably figure that, as long as a sizable share of Soviet forces remain survivable, the United States will be deterred from striking at the vulnerable elements. Second, the Soviets already have a large number of operational ICBMs with hard-target capability, and thus the acquisition of comparable systems like the MX would not give the United States a unilateral advantage. Third, the Soviet approach to force survivability has placed less importance than ours on the capability to "ride out" an adversary's attack and more on the capability to preempt in a crisis or to launch on warning (or launch under attack). Fourth, the Soviets probably judged that the price they would have to pay for heading off U.S. counterforce capabilities would have involved major limits on their own counterforce systems, a sacrifice they have been unwilling to make. And fifth, unlike the strategic implications of such advanced-technology programs as ballistic missile defense (BMD), ASAT, or antisubmarine warfare (ASW), the implications of U.S. counterforce programs are fairly predictable and can be taken into account with higher confidence in Soviet force planning. In particular, the Soviets have already committed themselves to reducing the share of their strategic forces located in fixed silos – and thus reducing their vulnerability to U.S. counterforce systems – by developing two new solid-fueled ICBMs (the SSX-24 and SSX-25) both capable of being deployed in mobile launchers as well as in silos.[10]

Thus the relatively low priority assigned to preventing U.S. hard-target-kill capabilities through arms control does not mean the Soviets were unconcerned by the military implications of such systems as the MX and D-5. Instead, it reflects their calculation that they were in a relatively better position to deal with those implications and serve overall Soviet interests through unilateral defense efforts than through arms control.

The Soviets have also appeared to assign a relatively low priority to constraining a range of other U.S. programs, including the B-1 bomber, the Trident submarine, the C-4 SLBM, improvements in air defenses, and upgraded command, control, and communications (C³) capabilities. Some of these other programs were criticized publicly by the Soviets for propaganda purposes (to demonstrate that the United States was "whipping up the arms race"); some the Soviets made rather brief and ritualistic attempts to ban in arms control negotiations; and some they simply ignored. But judging from the lack of sustained Soviet interest in prohibiting or, in some cases, even limiting these programs in arms control agreements, it is doubtful that any of these other U.S. programs have ranked very high on the Soviet hierarchy of concerns.

Eliminating vs. Limiting U.S. Threats

The Soviets have drawn distinctions among new U.S. programs and have been particularly interested in arms control constraints in those areas where they were not in a strong position to compete, such as advanced technology programs. In these cases, their preferred arms control solution has usually been to eliminate a challenging new U.S. capability altogether — before it has become a tested, operational system — rather than simply to restrict the size of the program. Their motivation in seeking such comprehensive solutions has been to proscribe whole areas of competition where they could be placed at a disadvantage, where planning would be difficult, and where large commitments of Soviet resources would be required. This motivation has led to Soviet proposals to ban all long-range cruise missiles (especially SLCMs and GLCMs), to rule out any deployment whatsoever of modern U.S. INF missiles in Western Europe, and to prohibit all ASAT capabilities. Similarly, although the ABM Treaty does not comprehensively ban missile defenses (in that it permits one ABM complex per side), it does prohibit the deployment of a nationwide ABM capability and therefore eliminates the uncertainties about the future effectiveness of Soviet offensive capabilities that had motivated the Soviets to seek limits on U.S. missile defenses.

In the event that such efforts to ban a new U.S. program do not prove negotiable, however, Soviet incentives to constrain the program may change substantially. Once they resign themselves to entering into (or, perhaps more likely, continuing) the competition in an area they realize will not be banned—especially once they commit additional resources and undertake additional programs to offset the new U.S. capability—the Soviets may well place less importance on limiting that competition than they had earlier placed on avoiding it altogether.

Of course, the Soviets would prefer that the new U.S. capability not go unconstrained. They can therefore be expected to see some value in negotiating limits on programs that they had originally hoped to ban. But having failed to close off an unpromising channel of competition and recognizing that their comparative advantage is in quantity rather than quality, the Soviets may be fairly relaxed about what those limits should be. Indeed, as far as the size of a new U.S. program is concerned, a critical threshold for them will often be zero. Once that threshold is crossed, their interest in limiting that program through negotiations may drop off considerably—and so may the price they are willing to pay (in terms of constraints on their own capabilities) to limit it.

Such a threshold appears to exist in the area of INF. For both political and military reasons, the Soviets have so far rejected any agreement that would permit even a single U.S. cruise or Pershing missile to be stationed in Western Europe. Presumably they see some military benefit in getting the United States to stop short of the planned level of 572. But it is not yet clear whether they would regard some number of U.S. missiles between 0 and 572 as a sufficient improvement over the situation that would exist in the absence of an agreement to pay a substantial price for such a result. Although the Soviets are surely not indifferent to increases in U.S. deployments from 1 to 572, the increment of greatest concern to them—and the one they would probably pay a disproportionate amount to block—is the increment between zero and one.

Soviet treatment of ALCMs in SALT II and START also illustrates how the negotiating priorities of the Soviets may change when and if they fail in their effort to ban a challenging new system. Not only did they attach less importance to achieving tight constraints on ALCMs than they originally attached to banning them, but their interest in limiting ALCMs did not differ markedly from their interest in limiting other programs permitted under the agreement, including those they had not earlier attempted to ban.

After initially proposing to prohibit long-range ALCMs in both negotiations, the Soviets later supported an approach that gave each side broad freedom, within certain numerical ceilings, to choose its own mix of weapons allowed by the agreement and thus to acquire large numbers of ALCMs, if it so desired, at the expense of other strategic weapons. Although the United States insisted on sublimits to impose special restrictions on particular categories of weapons such as heavy ICBMs and MIRVed ICBMs, the Soviets did not insist on comparable restrictions on ALCMs. Indeed, the limits on ALCMs supported by the Soviets were less restrictive than those agreed on for ballistic missile warheads.[11]

What this demonstrates is that the greater Soviet interest in banning U.S. ALCMs than banning, for example, U.S. counterforce ballistic missiles did not necessarily reflect the judgment that U.S. ALCMs would be any more capable or threatening than the MX or D-5. Instead, it simply reflected the judgment by the Soviets that, given the U.S. qualitative edge in cruise missile technology as well as the costs and uncertainties involved in seeking to offset the U.S. ALCM threat, it would be advantageous for them to head off a competition in ALCMs while at the same time competing on more favorable grounds (i.e., counterforce ballistic missiles).

Once the Soviets failed to head off that competition, they lost much of their interest in singling out ALCMs from other systems for more restrictive limits. First, as their own cruise missile programs progressed and as their air defense capability against small, low-flying missiles improved, both the potential U.S. advantage from ALCMs and the Soviet "need" for strict limits decreased. Second, once the introduction of ALCMs became inevitable, the more relevant comparison for the Soviets in determining their negotiating priorities was not between U.S. and Soviet ALCMs, but between the threat posed by U.S. ALCMs and the threat posed by U.S. ballistic missiles. Based on their SALT and START positions, it appears that the Soviets do not find U.S. ALCMs any more threatening than U.S. ballistic missile capabilities. They may well find them less so.

Thus, once their effort to ban ALCMs proved infeasible, the Soviets were prepared to lump them together with other systems to be permitted in SALT/START, even to treat them less restrictively than most of the others. Still, their interest in limiting ALCMs did not disappear. Indeed, the U.S. ALCM program continues to provide incentives for the Soviets to accept limits on their own strategic capabilities. But those incentives for constraining U.S. ALCM deployments are based at least as much on the large size of the program — and on its implications for overall numerical balances — as they are on the qualitative characteristics of U.S. ALCMs.

Incentives to Restrict Existing Programs

It has primarily been the United States that has been interested in limitations or reductions of existing weapon systems (including systems not yet deployed that would be permitted under an agreement). Although not normally the initiator of proposals for such limitations, the Soviet Union has nonetheless often been prepared to accept trade-offs involving existing capabilities provided the trade-offs were not detrimental to Soviet interests. One of the key factors influencing Soviet attitudes toward such trade-offs — and affecting the terms of the trade-offs themselves — has been the numerical size of U.S. defense programs.

Of course, the numerical size of U.S. programs is not always a critical factor in arms control. In the case of chemical weapons (CW), for example, it is probably the existence of a credible, usable U.S. CW deterrent capability, more than the size of U.S. CW stocks, that provides incentives for the Soviets to agree to mutual limitations. Even though the USSR is believed to possess numerically much larger stocks of CW agent, both sides maintain that an agreement should ban all CW stocks, not limit their size, despite the fact that the USSR would probably be required to destroy a much larger quantity of chemical weapons than would the United States.

Even in negotiations in which constraints are expressed in terms of numerical limitations in one or more categories of military capability (e.g., SALT, START, INF, Mutual and Balanced Force Reductions [MBFR] in Europe), numbers are never all-important. In evaluating any proposals put forward by the United States, the Soviets will naturally look at the interaction between quality and quantity. For example, they would be more interested in a U.S. offer to trade away 100 Pershing IIs as compared to 100 Pershing Is (which cannot reach Soviet territory), or 100 D-5 SLBMs as compared to 100 of the less powerful and accurate C-4 SLBMs. Similarly, in assessing a U.S. proposal for reductions in a weapons category such as ballistic missile warheads containing a variety of different systems, the Soviets would want to consider the types of weapons the United States would be expected to reduce under the proposal as compared with the types the Soviets would choose to reduce.

Thus, quantity can never really be divorced from quality. Nonetheless, especially in agreements containing numerical limits, sheer numbers may often carry considerable weight in the bargaining process, perhaps more than they deserve. The larger the numerical size of U.S. programs and deployments, the greater will be the available U.S. stock of bargaining capital. And the more numerous that stock of negotiating assets relative to corresponding Soviet assets, the greater will be the opportunity for achieving U.S. negotiating objectives. This will be the case however the United States seeks to use its quantitative leverage — whether it tries to cap Soviet weapons totals at a certain level by offering to cap U.S. totals at the same (or a different) level, to reduce Soviet totals by offering to reduce U.S. totals by the same or different amounts, or simply to barter away U.S. systems for comparable Soviet systems, such as the MX for SS-18s or U.S. INF missiles for SS-20s.

Soviet Numerical Momentum

It is in this area of numbers, however — as compared to the realm of technological innovation — where the U.S. bargaining position has been relatively weak. Over the last two decades, the Soviets have been engaged in a massive, across-the-board buildup in military capabilities, and nowhere has the quantitative momentum of that buildup been more impressive than in the category of strategic nuclear forces. The Soviets have now surpassed the United States in many of the familiar numerical indicators of strategic capability including, significantly, a number of categories that have become key units of limitation in arms control negotiations: strategic delivery vehicles, ICBMs, heavy ICBMs, MIRVed ICBMs, ICBM warheads, SLBMs, and ballistic missile warheads and throw-weight.

During this period, the United States was also adding to its strategic strength, and it has maintained numerical advantages in several categories of strategic capability on which it has traditionally relied more heavily than the Soviet Union. In particular, it continues to hold a numerical lead in SLBM warheads, heavy bombers, bomber weapons, and bomber payload, and these leads have enabled the United States to retain its advantage in the total number of strategic weapons — ballistic missile warheads and bomber weapons — one of the most important aggregate indicators of strategic capability.

But in evaluating negotiating leverage, it is essential to look not just at numerical balances at the time of negotiations, but also at how those balances are likely to evolve in the future in the absence of agreement. Trends are therefore important, and clearly the momentum has been on the Soviet side. A key source of this momentum in the field of strategic arms was the design and testing during the early and mid-1970s of the fourth generation of Soviet ICBMs (SS-17, SS-18, SS-19), which are MIRVed missiles with powerful boosters capable of carrying substantially more warheads than existing or planned U.S. ICBMs. The introduction of these large throw-weight ICBMs, together with Soviet development a few years later of MIRVed SLBMs, meant that it was just a matter of time before the Soviets would surpass the United States in ballistic warheads (ICBM warheads plus SLBM warheads) and then threaten the once-commanding U.S. lead in total strategic weapons. Currently, with the deployment of Trident submarines and ALCMs, the United States is managing to hang on to a lead of more than 1,000 total weapons. But with the Soviets expanding their edge in ballistic missile warheads and pursuing new bomber and ALCM programs of their own, it is uncertain whether and how long that lead will last.[12] (See Figures 1, 2, 3, and 4.)

FIGURE 1
U.S. and Soviet ICBM Launcher and Reentry Vehicle (RV) Deployment (1968–1984)

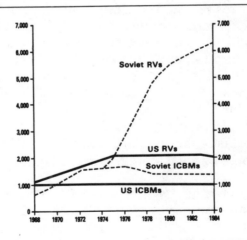

Source: U.S. Department of Defense, *Soviet Military Power, 1984* (Washington, D.C.: GPO, 1984), 24.

FIGURE 2
U.S. and Soviet SLBM Launcher and Reentry Vehicle (RV) Deployment (1968–1984)

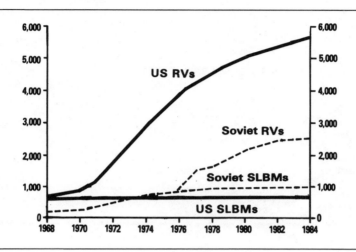

Source: U.S. Department of Defense, *Soviet Military Power, 1984* (Washington, D.C.: GPO, 1984), 26.

Thus, the quantitative trends in the strategic arms competition have been moving in the Soviet direction. And what is just as important, the Soviets have had the expectation – probably ever since the days of SALT I when their fourth-generation ICBMs were on the drawing boards – that the various strategic balances would evolve as they have. Because of the public nature of the U.S. defense planning and budgetary process, they have had a fairly good basis for projecting years into the future the U.S. side of the strategic equation. The Soviets have been able to reach the judgment that, in the absence of agreement, the United States would not be in a position credibly to threaten a numerical buildup that they would have difficulty matching, given their ongoing programs and open production lines. So, despite continuing U.S. advantages in several important areas of the strategic competition, the greater Soviet numerical momentum has been a critical part of the setting in which negotiations have taken

FIGURE 3
Strategic Nuclear Force—Modernization Comparison
(Introduction of Selected Systems by Year)

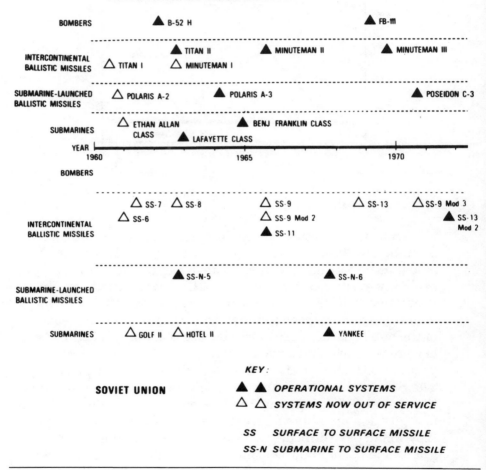

O B-1B

MINUTEMAN III   O PEACEKEEPER
(MK 12A)   (MX)

TRIDENT I (C-4)

OHIO CLASS

| 1975 | 1980 | 1985 |

BACKFIRE   BEAR H   O BLACKJACK

SS 11 Mod 2   SS-17 Mod 2   SS-19 Mod 3   O SS-X-25

SS-11 Mod 3   SS-18 Mod 2   O SS-X-24

SS-18 △   △ SS-17 △ SS-18 Mod 3   SS-17 Mod 3

△ SS-19   □ SS-16   SS-18 Mod 4

SS-19 MOD 2

SS-N-8   SS-N-18   SS-N-20   O SS-NX-23

SS-N-6 Mod 2   SS-N-18 Mod 2

SS-N-6 Mod 3   SS-N-8 Mod 2   SS-N-18   SS-N-17
                                Mod 3

DELTA I   DELTA II   DELTA III   TYPHOON

YANKEE II

O O *SYSTEMS IN FLIGHT TEST*

□ *SS-16 OPERATIONALLY CAPABLE. AVAILABLE
INFORMATION DOES NOT ALLOW CONCLUSIVE
JUDGEMENT ON WHETHER THE SOVIET UNION
HAS DEPLOYED THE SS-16 BUT DOES INDICATE
PROBABLE DEPLOYMENT.*

Source: NATO Information Service, *NATO and the Warsaw Pact: Force Comparisons* (Brussels: NATO, 1984), 27.

FIGURE 4
Strategic Forces (Trends in Relative Advantages between NATO and Warsaw Pact Forces)

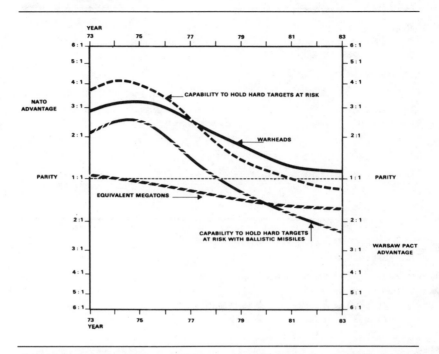

Source: NATO Information Service, *NATO and the Warsaw Pact: Force Comparisons* (Brussels: NATO, 1984), 29.

place and has had adverse implications for U.S. negotiating leverage.

U.S. Efforts to Limit Existing Forces

Despite the adverse quantitative trends, the United States has tried over the past 15 years to achieve ambitious objectives in arms control negotiations. In particular, it has attempted to halt or reverse Soviet quantitative momentum in weapons categories of concern to the United States, such as large MIRVed ICBMs. In a substantial number of cases, the United States proposed equal ceilings in categories in which the Soviets had already amassed a numerical lead or were well on their way to achieving one. In those cases where the United States proposed a common ceiling above the existing or planned U.S. level, its impact would have been exclusively on the Soviets. In other cases where the proposed ceiling fell below U.S. deployment levels or plans, the United States too would have been affected, but not as much as the Soviets. To help the Soviets swallow the idea of accepting larger constraints in weapon categories of primary importance to them, the U.S. proposals sometimes included constraints on U.S. systems of concern to Moscow. But often those compensating constraints would have had only a marginal impact on U.S. plans and were of only marginal interest to the Soviets.

The United States recognized that it was asking the Soviet Union in several negotiations to bear a greater share of the burden of constraints. But U.S. negotiators genuinely believed that reducing asymmetries in certain key weapon categories was essential to obtain a more stable balance of forces. In strategic arms control negotiations, for example, the United States maintained that weapons best suited for carrying out surprise attacks against an adversary's forces — particularly powerful and accurate MIRVed ICBMs — were highly destabilizing and should be subject to the strictest limits. Weapons with much longer flight times — bombers and cruise missiles — were retaliatory in nature and need not be constrained as severely. The fact that these U.S. judgments on the requirements of stability provided a rationale for proposing more stringent limits on Soviet forces than on U.S. forces did not, in the U.S. view, make them any less valid.

Notwithstanding the U.S. conviction that its proposals would promote stability and serve the broader interests of both sides, U.S. efforts during the past 15 years to narrow or eliminate Soviet advantages in weapon categories of importance to the USSR have not been very successful. As illustrated by the following examples, the Soviets have been prepared to accept modest limits on existing capabilities the United States considered destabilizing, but only on terms they considered equitable.

In the SALT I Interim Agreement the United States originally sought equal numerical limits that would have stopped Soviet building programs, including that for the heavy SS-9 ICBM, well short of plans.[13] But because the United States had no building programs in place that could have increased its number of ballistic missile launchers during the five-year duration of the agreement, it was not in a strong position to threaten a buildup in launchers in the absence of an agreement. It therefore eventually settled for a freeze on the number of launchers that were operational or under construction at the time of signature of the agreement. The result was to codify a substantial Soviet numerical lead in ballistic missile launchers, but a lead not as large as the Soviets probably would have achieved without the freeze. Indeed, there was evidence that the Soviets were preparing for an SS-9 force considerably larger than the number frozen by SALT I.

Considering that the five-year agreement did not alter any U.S. plans or programs (either the U.S. launcher production schedule or U.S. Minuteman III and Poseidon MIRVing programs) it might be asked why the Soviets agreed even to modest constraints on their buildup. Part of the explanation is that the Soviets had important nonmilitary reasons for concluding SALT I (discussed in a later chapter). But the factor most widely viewed as responsible for Moscow's acceptance of the Interim Agreement's constraints, especially on the SS-9, was the strong Soviet interest in obtaining the limits on U.S. missile defense capabilities imposed by the ABM Treaty, which the administration linked to the conclusion of the Interim Agreement on offensive arms.[14] Thus, to the extent that U.S defense programs (rather than foreign policy and other nonmilitary considerations) provided incentives for the Soviets to accept modest constraints on their offensive capabilities in SALT I, what seems responsible was the qualitative threat posed by the U.S. ABM capabilities rather than the negligible quantitative leverage the United States possessed because of the absence of active launcher production programs.

In SALT II, again from a relatively weak position quantitatively, the United States sought to narrow or eliminate Soviet numerical leads in certain key measures of strategic capability. The U.S. proposal of March 1977, for example, called for a ceiling of between 1,800 and 2,000 strategic delivery vehicles, which would have required U.S. reductions of at least 283 mostly nonoperational systems and Soviet reductions of at least 504 operational but aging systems[15]; a sublimit of 550 MIRVed ICBMs, which would have required a reduction in planned Soviet systems of more than 370 but would have had a much smaller impact on U.S. plans[16]; and a further sublimit of 150 heavy ICBMs, which would have reduced the 308 Soviet SS-18s by more than half and not affected the United States, which did not possess comparable missiles. Despite the fact that the March 1977 initiative offered to give up the MX program and contained some other concessions presumably of interest to the Soviets, they rejected the proposal, arguing in part that it called on them to bear a grossly unequal share of the sacrifices.

Eventually the United States got a small part of the loaf it asked for in March 1977. In particular, the Soviets agreed to a delivery vehicle ceiling of 2,250, requiring them to reduce by about 250 and the United States by none. The Soviets also agreed to a sublimit of 820 MIRVed ICBMs, resulting in no change in U.S. plans but about 100 fewer such Soviet missiles than they probably would otherwise have deployed. But these Soviet concessions did not come for free. They were elements of the September 1977 package deal, referred to above, in which the United States accepted various quantitative and qualitative constraints on its cruise missile programs. And despite these Soviet concessions on ceilings for delivery vehicles and MIRVed ICBMs, the Soviets did not budge on heavy ICBMs, insisting on no reduction in their deployment of 308.

Soviet behavior in INF has been consistent with long-standing Soviet reluctance to surrender quantitative advantages without receiving what they consider to be adequate compensation. In November 1981, President Ronald Reagan announced that the United States would abandon its planned deployment of 572 INF missiles if the Soviet Union would destroy all comparable missiles. Thus, in exchange for a cut of 572 Western INF warheads yet to be deployed, this "zero-zero" option would have required a Soviet reduction, at that time, of more than 1,000 deployed INF warheads. While strongly supporting the idea of zero on the U.S. side, the Soviets strenuously objected to the total dismantling worldwide of Soviet INF missiles, arguing that Soviet systems were needed to balance British, French, and Chinese forces. Later, the United States modified its proposal by calling for reductions to an equal number of INF warheads for both the United States and USSR. The Soviets, however, continued to insist on no U.S. deployments and to agree only to reduce Soviet INF forces targeted against Europe to a number equivalent to UK and French forces.

Before walking out of the INF talks in November 1983, the Soviets indicated they could agree to a reduction of 572 Soviet warheads targeted against Europe and a freeze on deployments in Asia if the United States agreed to an equal reduction of 572 (that is, if it abandoned its deployments altogether). NATO rejected the idea together with its premise of denying the United States the right to proceed with deployments. When and if the Soviets come around to accepting the deployment of some Western INF missiles, they will be very reluctant to concede that U.S. and Soviet levels should be equal, either globally or in Europe. This is mainly because of the greater reductions the Soviets would be required to make to get to equal levels, but also because they have staked out such a firm public position that British and French forces must be counted in the Western totals.

The Vienna-based MBFR talks, which are primarily concerned with NATO and Warsaw Pact troop levels in Central Europe, also demonstrate Soviet unwillingness to bear an unequal burden of sacrifice in arms control agreements. The primary NATO negotiating objective in MBFR has been to eliminate the Warsaw Pact's large and destabilizing advantage in military manpower in Central Europe. Accordingly, the Western participants proposed an equal ceiling of 700 thousand ground force personnel for both sides as well as an equal ceiling of 900 thousand combined ground and air personnel for both sides. As in several of the nuclear negotiations, the United States was asking the Soviets to accept unequal reductions to arrive at a balance we considered more stable and equitable. And just as in the other negotiations, the Soviets claimed that the existing balance was already equitable, and that asymmetrical reductions would only serve to upset that balance.

The initial Warsaw Pact proposal amounted to 17 percent reductions for both sides and was designed to leave the existing ratio of forces unchanged. In June 1978, the Warsaw Pact finally accepted the Western proposal for common ceilings at 700 thousand and 900 thousand, but with an important proviso—reductions would have to be carried out on the basis of Eastern bloc data on existing force levels. The joker in the Soviet deck was revealed when the Soviets tabled their data. Although Soviet estimates of NATO forces were close to the figures submitted by the West on its own forces, Soviet data on Warsaw Pact forces were more than 150 thousand below Western estimates.[17] Moreover, according to Soviet estimates, existing NATO and Warsaw Pact totals were just about equal, so both sides could reach the common ceilings by making approximately equal reductions. Ever since June 1978 the discrepancy over data has been the principal stumbling block in the MBFR negotiations.

In each of these cases, the Soviets were prepared to accept limits on their existing capabilities, but not on terms the United States initially proposed. Not unexpectedly, they have strenuously rejected the concepts of stability and balance on which the United States has based its proposals for unequal Soviet sacrifices. They have argued, for instance, that the division of weapon systems into more and less destabilizing categories was contrived by the United States to

justify placing stringent limits on weapons traditionally relied upon by the USSR and more permissive limits on those
preferred by the United States.

While attacking U.S. views on stability and balance, the
Soviets have put forward their own concept of balance – based
on the vague and subjective notion they call "equality and
equal security" – under which the USSR is entitled to compensation for a wide range of unilateral advantages supposed-
ly conferred on the United States by geographic asymmetries,
technological strengths, and alliance relationships. On the
basis of their approach to nuclear accounting, the Soviets
have contended that, throughout the period the United States
was putting forward its one-sided proposals, parity had existed in central strategic forces, intermediate range forces,
and NATO-Warsaw Pact conventional forces in Central Europe. They argued that, if parity existed in advance of agreement, then the only way to arrive at a new level of parity
would be for both sides to give up equal capability – not for
the USSR, as Washington had proposed, to make unequal
sacrifices.

Obviously, we can only speculate on the extent to which
Soviet arguments about stability and parity reflect actual
Soviet perceptions of military balances and the extent to
which they are tactical devices to help preserve Soviet advantages. Both factors are probably present, although in
varying degrees in each case. In assessing the strategic balance, for example, the Soviets probably recognize that, given
the formidable air defenses faced by U.S. bombers and cruise
missiles compared to the virtual absence of defenses confront-
ing ballistic missile warheads (due to the ABM Treaty), it
does not make sense to equate such warheads and bomber
weapons on a one-for-one basis. On the other hand, the Soviets presumably have a healthy respect for the ability of
U.S. bombers and cruise missiles to penetrate to their targets
and would oppose any arms control approach that treated
them as benign in comparison to ballistic missiles.

In the INF context, the Soviets are no doubt genuinely
concerned about plans for the modernization and expansion

of third party forces, if not about the current levels of those forces. But they must recognize, at the same time, that equating U.S., British, and French SLBMs is not a realistic means of measuring NATO's deterrent capabilities and that, even if their argument for counting U.K. and French forces were granted, the Warsaw Pact would still have a large superiority in INF capabilities. In general, Soviet arguments about parity in intermediate-range nuclear forces and in conventional forces in Central Europe have a more hollow ring than their assertions about parity in central strategic capabilities.

In terms of negotiating behavior, however, it may make little difference whether the Soviets genuinely believe that parity exists or whether they believe they have a numerical edge. The Soviets are acutely sensitive both to the political as well as the military implications of numerical balances (or imbalances) and can be expected in negotiations to try to preserve and, if possible, to improve their relative quantitative position vis-à-vis the United States — whether that position is one of parity or superiority. In either case, they will resist U.S. proposals that they believe call on them to make disproportionately greater sacrifices. Perhaps if they truly believe that parity exists and that a U.S. proposal would leave them at a serious disadvantage, they would be especially dogged in their resistance. But even if they felt they enjoyed a comfortable edge, they would not be very keen on surrendering it without receiving suitable compensation.

The cases cited above support the conclusion that the Soviets are not inclined to provide the United States with a free lunch. Indeed, they have appeared consistently to follow a negotiating principle of equivalent sacrifices — no Soviet cuts or limits without constraints of comparable magnitude on the U.S. side. The initial U.S. proposals in each case clearly did not meet the test of equivalent sacrifice. Moreover, given the greater relative momentum of Soviet programs throughout much of the period, Soviet negotiators recognized that, in the absence of agreement, the likelihood of the United States reducing Soviet advantages through U.S. defense programs was remote. Accordingly, the Soviets felt they had little incentive to agree to what they regarded as one-sided deals.

Nonetheless, the Soviets were prepared to accept more modest constraints on their capabilities in exchange for what they considered to be fair compensation. Where the incentives provided by existing U.S. forces were not sufficient, they were supplemented by constraints on new U.S. capabilities. Thus, Soviet interest in limiting U.S. ABM capabilities was instrumental in obtaining modest limits on Soviet offensive forces in SALT I. And in SALT II, certain qualitative limits on cruise missiles, including the moratorium on GLCM and SLCM deployments, supplemented U.S. quantitative leverage (including the modest numerical constraints placed on ALCMs) in obtaining Soviet reductions in the planned number of MIRVed ICBMs and in strategic delivery vehicles.

U.S. Defense Programs and Soviet Incentives

The opportunity to limit U.S. defense programs is, to a large extent, what motivates the Soviets to accept negotiated limits on their own military capabilities. Without that opportunity, there would be little promise of meaningful arms control. But the incentives for Soviet negotiating concessions will vary considerably from case to case and will often be quite limited.

The Soviets have had a much stronger interest in heading off new U.S. programs and capabilities than limiting the size of existing ones. But not all new U.S. programs have stimulated the Soviets to give a high priority to arms control. Some programs have simply not generated serious military concern and have not required much in the way of offsetting Soviet actions. Others have generated greater military concern, but the Soviets have found themselves in a relatively good position to offset the effects of those programs without arms control. In the case of still other programs, however, the USSR has seen considerable advantage in averting what appeared to be a costly, unpredictable, and disadvantageous competition. It is to this category of new programs that Soviet arms control proposals and energies have largely been devoted. And it is from these programs that the United States derives the most potential negotiating leverage. But if the United States is not prepared, for whatever reasons, to forgo the program of concern to the Soviets, Soviet interest in constraining its size may decline precipitately, together with Soviet incentives for limiting their own capabilities.

Compared with their interest in blocking entirely new channels of arms competition, the Soviets have given a much lower priority to seeking restrictive limits on the size of programs that will be permitted under agreements. Regarding such permitted systems, the principal Soviet arms control objective has been to ensure that they do not adversely affect the existing overall numerical relationship between U.S. and Soviet forces. But given the greater Soviet quantitative momentum over the last 15 years, the Soviets have rarely felt challenged by U.S. numbers. This is not to say that existing programs have not provided useful bargaining assets. The Soviets have seen benefits in trade-offs that constrain U.S. and Soviet numbers. But they have been under little pressure to accept such limits on terms they considered disadvantageous.

The limited numbers of forces the United States was able and willing to put on the negotiating table during the past 15 years have clearly been a handicap in achieving U.S. negotiating objectives—especially because U.S. arms control proposals during that period often had the very ambitious goal of eliminating worrisome force asymmetries that the United States was not prepared to eliminate through unilateral U.S. defense efforts. Given Soviet resistance to arms control trade-offs that do not involve U.S. sacrifices at least equivalent to their own, it is worth considering whether the mixed negotiating record could have been improved if the United States had been prepared to put more of its available negotiating assets on the table.

For example, in the area of strategic arms where—at least on a simple, bean-counting basis—there is rough equality in the number of weapons, could the United States have obtained more restrictive limits on Soviet ballistic missile capabilities if it had been willing to accept substantial cutbacks in its bomber or ALCM programs, as opposed to the permissive limits of SALT II that readily accommodated planned deployments? Probably it could have done somewhat better. But there have been, and will continue to be, strong arguments for not putting all U.S. bargaining assets on the table. In the case of bombers and ALCMs, the United States has been strongly committed to maintaining the effectiveness of the bomber leg of the triad in the face of a vast Soviet lead in air defenses, and this has required "air-breathing" forces in substantial numbers.

As discussed above, the potentially most powerful U.S. negotiating leverage comes from the Soviet interest in banning altogether a new and challenging U.S. capability; but that leverage may drop off rapidly if the United States is not prepared to accept a total ban. This may confront us with difficult choices. But often the United States will decide that overall U.S. interests are better served by forfeiting potential negotiating leverage and proceeding as planned with our programs. In INF, for example, maximum U.S. negotiating leverage would come from agreeing not to deploy any U.S. missiles in Western Europe. But there were strong reasons, such as the need for deployments to "couple" the defense of Europe to the U.S. strategic deterrent, to forgo the potential leverage the United States could obtain from a total ban. In a variety of other cases such as forward-based aircraft in SALT and UK and French systems in INF, the United States has similarly chosen to pass up the use of some available bargaining assets for the sake of broader goals.

This is not to say that U.S. reticence to part with its systems at the negotiating table is always justified. But the argument illustrates that not all U.S. potential negotiating capital will always be usable. To have bargaining leverage, it is not enough to have active defense programs—it is necessary to be in a position to bargain with them.

Another question worth trying to answer is whether the United States could have done better at limiting Soviet ballistic missile forces if the quantitative momentum of U.S. programs had been greater throughout the past 15 years. It seems very likely that, if the numerical ratio of U.S. to Soviet forces had been more favorable, the United States could have attained a somewhat better result. But increasing U.S. numbers would not necessarily have produced a more favorable ratio; it might simply have stimulated more Soviet production and higher Soviet numbers that would have preserved the original ratio. Clearly, quantitative arms racing is where the Soviets have a comparative advantage, and they have demonstrated little hesitation about competing in that domain. Whether or not the Soviets would have tried to preserve their relative position through additional deployments of their own might have varied from case to case on the basis of their perceptions of the balance. If they believed there was parity, they would be expected to match any U.S. buildup. If they believed they were ahead, they might still want to retain their favorable position—but the impetus to build would not be as strong.

Finally, it should be recognized that, even if the United States had been willing and able to put more U.S. negotiating assets on the table in the interest of achieving its goals (whether by building more than it did or by being willing to part with more of what was already available or planned), it is by no means certain that the Soviets would have been prepared to cut back their ballistic missile capabilities, even on a basis they would have regarded as equitable. That would depend on the extent to which the Soviets, regardless of considerations of balance, valued those capabilities and considered them essential for their own strategic purposes—a subject to be covered in the next chapter.

3

The USSR's Attitude Toward
Constraining Its Own Capabilities

To assess U.S. negotiating leverage, it is not sufficient to focus on Soviet interest in constraining U.S. defense programs. Soviet interest in halting or limiting U.S. programs gives the Soviets an incentive to accept constraints on their own capabilities. But whether that incentive will be strong enough to produce an agreement, or progress toward an agreement, will depend to a large extent on how they view the concessions the United States asks them to make – and how they view the trade-off between those concessions and the benefits they would hope to achieve from reciprocal limits placed on the United States.

Arms Control in Soviet Strategic Planning

The idea of promoting the security of the Soviet state through arms control does not come naturally to Soviet leaders. They tend to take the traditional military view – not uncommon among governments and military establishments throughout the world, including in the United States – that national security should be based on unilateral defense efforts, not on arrangements negotiated with adversaries. Accordingly, the overriding priority of Soviet defense planners is to develop and acquire the weapon systems deemed necessary to serve Soviet military requirements. The planning process seems to be carried out independently of arms control considerations, without counting on successful negotiations to help solve critical security problems.

An example of this attitude has been the approach toward remedying the growing vulnerability of Soviet strategic assets, including fixed ICBMs and command and control facilities, to U.S. nuclear attack. The Soviets have devoted little attention to promoting the survivability of these assets through negotiated constraints on the U.S. counterforce threat — that is, by seeking to ban the types or limit the numbers of U.S. systems that most threaten Soviet forces. Instead, they have gone about fixing the problem unilaterally and at great expense by developing mobile ICBMs, fortifying missile silos and command posts against nuclear blast, and so on.

The United States has also pursued such unilateral efforts to promote survivability, including the multiple protective shelter basing scheme under President Jimmy Carter and current plans for the Midgetman small, mobile ICBM. But in addition, the United States has given greater emphasis than the Soviets to seeking arms control measures capable of constraining the threat to the survivability of U.S. forces. By constraining the Soviet threat, the United States has sought to make its unilateral survivability efforts more effective, less extensive and costly, or both. In Geneva, the United States told the Soviets, in effect, that the current vulnerability of U.S. ICBMs is the fault of the USSR and that, in order to restore stability, the USSR should agree to deep cuts in those Soviet systems that threaten U.S. forces. With incredulity that does not seem entirely feigned, Soviet negotiators have replied that they do not understand the basis for such a demand. The U.S. vulnerability problem, they have said, is the fault of the United States. The United States *allowed* its systems to become vulnerable. If the United States is so concerned about the problem, it should take the trouble to correct it, not complain to the Soviet Union.

The Soviet disavowal of responsibility for the vulnerability of U.S. forces is obviously both wrong and self-serving. But the notion that a superpower should look to its own capabilities and resources, rather than to arms control, to solve critical security problems appears to be deeply imbedded in the Soviet strategic psyche.

Moreover, the Soviet system of long-term planning tends to reinforce this preference for self-reliance. Once high-level planning decisions are taken, resources committed, and organizational and personal interests engaged, it can become very difficult to alter plans and programs, even more so than in the United States. The Soviet system does not respond very flexibly or rapidly to changed incentives and disincentives provided by U.S. defense programs and negotiating proposals. As experienced observers of Soviet defense planning have pointed out, "the Soviet system is barely capable of making marginal adjustments, let alone major shifts."[18] The rigidities of the Soviet defense planning and procurement process have made it difficult for arms control negotiations to have more than a marginal impact on ongoing Soviet defense programs.

The 1972 ABM Treaty is frequently cited as a case in which arms control, contrary to the norm, produced a major and sudden change in Soviet force plans. It is true that the treaty represented an about-face in the Soviet attitude toward constraints on defenses and a rare example of the Soviets not going forward with a military program on which they had already embarked. But the treaty itself did not actually halt an ongoing Soviet program; by the time the treaty was signed, Soviet ABM deployment plans were already in a state of suspended animation.

In the late 1960s, largely as a result of the serious technical shortcomings of the Galosh ABM system that had become increasingly evident since construction had begun at the start of the decade, the Soviets scaled back their ABM program substantially. Of the eight complexes that were originally to have constituted the Moscow ABM system, only four were eventually completed. Active construction had been started but abandoned at two sites. The truncated system probably became fully operational in 1970 or 1971, but the Soviets presumably regarded its utility as very limited. By then the decision seems to have been taken not to proceed with ABM defenses other than at Moscow for the time being. The Soviets may well have concluded that further ABM deployments would have to await significant improvements in technology.[19]

What the ABM Treaty did was to perpetuate and codify a self-imposed Soviet hiatus in additional ABM deployments. This is not to suggest that, in the absence of the treaty, the Soviets would have unilaterally abandoned ballistic missile defenses. Presumably they would have kept open the option to proceed with full-scale deployments when they judged that a technically effective system could be built. And it took the advent of the U.S. ABM program – with the threat that a technologically superior U.S. system could erode the Soviet deterrent capability – to persuade them to close that option formally. But it does suggest that the Soviets, in accepting the ABM Treaty, were not suddenly interrupting an ongoing program or abruptly modifying existing plans. Indeed, if the Galosh ABM program had been thriving in the late 1960s and there had been active plans for expanded deployments, it is not at all certain that the Soviets would have been inclined to negotiate the ABM Treaty, even with the strong incentives for mutual restraint provided by the inauguration of the U.S. program.

Thus, arms control has tended to have a marginal impact on Soviet forces and plans as a consequence of a Soviet strategic mindset that places paramount importance on unilateral defense programs in achieving vital security objectives and of a Soviet planning system that makes ongoing programs difficult to alter. Nonetheless, arms control has been viewed by Soviet leaders as a useful instrument of defense policy; but the role they have wanted it to play has been quite different from the role arms control has played in the United States. For the Soviets, the primary function of arms control is not to constrain or manipulate existing force structures; it is instead to codify existing U.S.-Soviet force relationships and to insulate existing forces and force plans from the shocks and surprises of new weapon developments. Having invested heavily in forces designed to serve their strategic objectives, the Soviets seek to use arms control to protect that investment against U.S. programs that could disrupt existing balances, nullify Soviet advantages, complicate Soviet planning, and undermine Soviet objectives. Arms control, in other words, plays a conservative role.

Of course the United States also attempts to protect its existing plans and forces during arms control negotiations. But its primary goal in such negotiations has usually been to revise the existing relationship between U.S. and Soviet forces to make it conform more closely to U.S. concepts of stability. In the process, it has sought major changes in the existing Soviet force structure. And although the United States has naturally preferred to obtain such changes without having to make important modifications in its own plans, it has nonetheless been prepared on occasion to compromise those plans to achieve its restructuring goals.[20]

The Soviets, too, are interested in achieving their goals on the cheap, perhaps by seeking to block a challenging new U.S. capability by offering to forgo an analogous Soviet program that is not likely to be a match for its U.S. counterpart. Past Soviet offers to ban cruise missiles and current Soviet interest in a ban on space systems fall in this category. But when the opportunity to limit a U.S. program of concern to them has meant having to pay a substantial price, especially in terms of cutting back existing forces of particular value to them, the Soviets have often lost their appetite for mutual limits. Given the choice between limiting U.S. programs through mutual constraints and protecting their own forces by avoiding arms control, the Soviets will often err on the side of protecting their own forces. As one U.S. expert has noted:

> Due to the Soviet Union's order of priorities, her leaders, much like defense planners and conservative analysts in the United States, tend to prefer a free hand for them-

selves, even if this means giving a free hand to the other side, rather than to constrain themselves in constraining the other side. Thus, they have never been much taken with the strategy of attempting to forestall the development of new or substantially enhanced American capabilities by mortgaging the future of their programs.[21]

For the Soviets, too much arms control is far worse than too little. They are more likely to reject a deal because it attempts to put too many constraints on them than because it places too few on the United States. Indeed, they will often prefer what in the United States is derisively called a "cosmetic" agreement.

In view of the rigidities of Soviet defense planning, as well as Soviet reluctance to trade away existing capabilities, the fact that the Soviets may have a strong interest in placing limits on particular U.S. programs is no guarantee that they will be willing, in exchange, to accept the limits the United States seeks on their forces. Nonetheless, on numerous occasions they have been prepared to agree to limits on Soviet capabilities in exchange for constraints on U.S. capabilities of roughly comparable importance. But the types of Soviet capabilities they have been willing to constrain – and those they have been very reluctant to constrain – have tended to reflect a hierarchy of Soviet military values and priorities.

Soviet Objectives and Negotiating Priorities

Perhaps the clearest case of negotiating behavior of the Soviet Union that reflects its military doctrine and objectives has been the Soviet approach to the protection of its modern ICBM capabilities.

The question of whether the Soviets believe a nuclear war can be won – and indeed whether they are seeking to acquire a war-winning capability – has for years been a source of heated debate in the West. Whatever the answers to these questions, the Soviets clearly believe, should nuclear war occur, that they must have on hand the strategic forces to fight it in a militarily effective manner and thus to limit as much as possible the U.S. ability to destroy the Soviet homeland. That has meant the ability to launch a prompt, massive attack, perhaps preemptively, against critical military targets in the United States, including fortified ICBM silos and command and control installations.

To Soviet planners, the forces most suitable for carrying out such an attack have been modern MIRVed ICBMs, with their numerous, powerful, and accurate warheads capable of destroying hard targets, their virtually continuous state of combat readiness, and their high degree of controllability. ICBMs have been the preferred systems not only because of their technical suitability but also because of a historic Soviet affinity for land-based rocket forces and a variety of geographic and technological factors that make sea-based forces a poor alternative for the USSR. On the basis of these considerations, the Soviets proceeded during the 1970s and early 1980s to develop and deploy their fourth-generation ICBMs, including the SS-17, the SS-19, and the 10-warhead "heavy" SS-18. Currently the Soviets have 818 such missiles with well over 5,000 warheads, about two-thirds of the total number of Soviet strategic weapons. This massive hard-target capability enables the Soviets to hold at risk virtually the entire range of strategic targets in the United States.

Perhaps the most consistent, and least successful, U.S. arms control objective over the last 15 years has been the effort to constrain this Soviet counterforce ICBM capability and, specifically, to prevent the Soviets from obtaining (and, later, to persuade them to reduce) the capability to threaten the U.S. silo-based ICBM force in a first strike. During SALT I, SALT II, and START, the United States tried almost every conceivable device to promote that objective—restrictions on heavy ICBMs, missile volume, silo dimensions, MIRVed ICBMs, MIRVed ICBM throw-weight, MIRVed heavy missiles, ICBM warheads, and so forth. As indicated earlier, these efforts were, at best, marginally successful. The Soviets were prepared, for a price, to accept constraints that capped their counterforce capabilities at high levels, probably somewhat below planned levels. But they strongly resisted substantial cuts in their modern ICBM capabilities and have insisted on protecting their capability to place U.S. fixed ICBMs and other vital strategic assets in jeopardy.

Obviously, we can only speculate on the reasons for persistent Soviet reluctance to cut back significantly on their ICBM capabilities. Several factors are probably responsible. The relative lack of momentum in U.S. strategic programs may have decreased Soviet incentives to meet U.S. demands. And the United States probably could have obtained somewhat better results if it had been willing to put more available bargaining assets on the table. But it seems reasonable to maintain that, even if the United States had been able and willing to offer the Soviets a substantially better deal, they would have insisted on retaining ICBM capabilities sufficient to carry out massive strikes against U.S. strategic targets.

Again, the March 1977 proposal is instructive. The Soviets had the opportunity to get rid of 200 prospective MX ICBMs and, with the proposed freeze on ICBM upgrades, to block a U.S. hard-target ICBM threat altogether. The Soviets no doubt regarded some elements of the proposal as one-sided and unacceptable, including the halt it would have imposed on their ICBM MIRVing programs. But why, if the Soviets were willing to reduce their counterforce assets in exchange for reasonable compensation, did they not make a counterproposal changing the elements they found troublesome? Why have they never offered to reduce their 308 heavy ICBMs for some price – even an outlandish price? Weren't there some strategic objectives the Soviets might have tried to achieve by meeting the United States halfway on its ICBM-related proposals – for example, a ban on cruise missiles in return for deep cuts in MIRVed ICBMS?

It seems that the Soviets were less interested in pursuing such deals than in retaining the forces deemed necessary to perform a central Soviet strategic mission. What this may demonstrate is that, at any given time, certain elements of the Soviet force structure may simply not be negotiable—at least not at any price that the United States would conceivably be willing to pay.

Does this mean that Soviet acquisition of the capability to destroy U.S. ICBM silos was inevitable—that there was no way we could have headed off such a capability through arms control? Probably not. If the United States had not begun its MIRV flight-test program in 1968 but instead had deferred testing while seeking a MIRV ban early in the SALT I talks, it is possible (but by no means certain) that the Soviets would have agreed to prohibit MIRVs and thereby made disarming strikes against ICBM silos impractical. And it is also conceivable that, early in the 1970s, the United States might have used its head start in MIRVing and its large lead in total strategic weapons as trading capital to try to cap Soviet ICBM MIRVing at a level far below what eventually materialized. But once the Soviets made sufficient progress on their fourth-generation ICBMs to have confidence that the capability to destroy U.S. fixed ICBMs was within their technological reach (perhaps in the mid-1970s), Soviet acquisition of such a capability may have become, for all intents and purposes, "inevitable."

Does Soviet resistence during the last 15 years to trading away counterforce ICBM capabilities mean that Soviet heavy ICBMs and other ICBM war-fighting assets will remain essentially non-negotiable for the foreseeable future? Again, probably not. But just as the Soviets may have been determined in the past to retain their capability to destroy U.S. hard targets almost regardless of the price the United States was willing to pay to limit that capability, Soviet willingness in the future to limit their large MIRVed ICBMs may have less to do with what the United States is prepared to offer in return than with how the Soviets see their own force requirements evolving in a changing strategic environment.

For example, U.S. replacement of part of its vulnerable, fixed-based ICBMs with harder-to-destroy mobile missiles could reduce some of the perceived war-fighting value of current Soviet MIRVed ICBMs and remove some of the incentive for retaining them in large numbers. Similarly, the introduction of U.S. hard-target-capable systems could induce the Soviets to deploy an increasing share of their ICBMs in mobile launchers and a decreasing share in vulnerable silos, and this could mean a reduction of large MIRVed ICBMs in favor of smaller, less threatening mobile systems. Moreover, regardless of deployments on the U.S. side, the Soviets might find that technological improvements (such as more accurate guidance systems and more efficient rocket fuels) will enable them to deploy smaller missiles with just as much combat effectiveness as the current generation of large ICBMs, and this could increase their receptivity to reducing the number of larger systems.[22] And, should the United States decide in the future to deploy advanced ballistic missile defenses, the Soviets might calculate that missile systems quite different from their current generation of ICBMs would be required to improve their prospects of penetrating such defenses.

Thus, depending on how they assess their changing strategic requirements, the Soviets may well negotiate more flexibly in the future on their ICBM capabilities than they did in the past. But greater Soviet flexibility on ICBMs would not necessarily mean that the Soviets had adopted a more receptive attitude toward arms control trade-offs—that they had become more interested in limiting existing U.S. capabilities and less interested in protecting their own. It would simply mean that there had been a change in the capabilities that their strategic objectives required them to protect.

This raises an important point about U.S. negotiating leverage. Given the Soviet inclination to forgo limitations on the United States if such limitations would involve trading away capabilities needed to achieve critical Soviet strategic objectives, the United States is more likely, in the case of certain weapon systems, to be able to influence Soviet negotiating behavior over the long term by altering the strategic context in which arms control trade-offs take place than it is in the short term by offering trade-offs that are marginally more generous to the USSR.

Thus, as long as Soviet MIRVed ICBMs can threaten

the U.S. ICBM force and are themselves invulnerable to U.S. attack, the Soviets will strenuously resist U.S. proposals to reduce their ICBM war-fighting capabilities. And although offering the Soviets a more attractive deal—such as more restrictive limits on U.S. bombers and cruise missiles—could result in somewhat lower limits on Soviet ICBMs, the Soviets would nonetheless be sure to leave themselves plenty of forces to carry out their desired counterforce missions. But if the United States can alter the value that the Soviets place on their own systems by making them vulnerable or adopting mobile basing that denies them their counterforce utility, then Soviet willingness to reduce their large ICBMs should increase substantially. It is in this sense that the deployment of U.S. mobile ICBMs and counterforce ballistic missiles such as the MX and D-5 can provide the United States with substantial negotiating leverage whether or not those systems are treated as bargaining assets and limited in the negotiating process.[23]

Other Soviet Sticking Points

Resistance to reducing ICBM capabilities is the most striking example of Soviet reluctance to make concessions in strategic arms negotiations. But the Soviets have persistently opposed some other kinds of U.S. negotiating demands, several of which were related to constraining Soviet ICBM forces.

For example, Soviet negotiators have vigorously opposed U.S. proposals in SALT and START that would have altered significantly their preferred mix of strategic forces, particularly by decreasing their reliance on ICBMs and moving toward sea-based and bomber capabilities. In this connection, the Soviets criticized the U.S. START proposal calling for separate limits on ballistic missiles and bombers, arguing that it would force them to reduce the systems they have traditionally relied on (i.e., ballistic missiles) while building up to the U.S. level in an area where they have no desire to match the United States (i.e., bombers). Such a "restructuring" of Soviet forces, they claim, would be extremely expensive. In addition, because it would reduce the most capable Soviet forces and build up in an area of comparative disadvantage, they assert that it would result in a serious net loss of military effectiveness. In this connection, reluctance to deploy a significantly larger proportion of strategic forces at sea seems to be based, in part, on concerns about the perceived vulnerability of Soviet submarines to U.S. ASW capabilities. And although the Soviets do not talk to us about their internal infighting, a change in the force mix would step on some powerful bureaucratic toes, including those of the Strategic Rocket Forces.

The Soviets firmly rejected the U.S. SALT II proposal to count the Backfire as a "heavy bomber," in part because of the force structuring implications of doing so. Having to include several hundred Backfires in the SALT II aggregate would have meant the displacement of several hundred other systems, particularly ballistic missiles. Over time, rather than being stuck with an aircraft that was counted as a strategic bomber but was neither optimized for that role nor actually performing it, the Soviets might have felt compelled at great cost to get rid of the Backfire, to develop a larger aircraft such as the Blackjack to perform the strategic mission, and to develop a new bomber of unambiguous intermediate range to perform Backfire's regional and naval missions.

The Soviets have also opposed U.S. proposals that have had the effect of blocking a promising new weapons program in an advanced stage of development. A key example of this was the repeated rejection of the proposal in SALT I to establish the boundary between "light" and "heavy" ICBMs at a level that would have precluded the SS-19 ICBM then being developed. The Soviets were counting on the SS-19 to be a mainstay of their MIRVed ICBM force. (They eventually deployed 360 of these six-warhead missiles.) If they had agreed to rule out the SS-19 in SALT, they would have either had to deploy a less satisfactory alternative (e.g., the less capable, four-warhead SS-17) or spend several additional years developing a substitute.

Another sticking point for the Soviet Union has involved U.S. proposals calling for the dismantling or destruction of weapon systems before the end of their useful lifetimes, particularly recently-deployed systems. The Soviets have argued that prematurely taking down operational systems would be an unacceptable waste of resources. Their objections to the two-thirds cut in deployed SS-18s proposed initially by the United States in START were based in part on this argument. Given the traditional Soviet reluctance to throw anything away, the Soviet INF "equal reductions" proposal, under which the Soviets would have destroyed more than 120 relatively new SS-20s and all remaining SS-4s stands out as a rare exception and provides an indication of how much they would like to stop NATO's Pershing and GLCM deployments.

Areas of Greater Flexibility

While strongly resisting concessions in certain areas, the Soviets have been prepared to accept limitations on existing capabilities in some other areas in the interest of obtaining compensating constraints on the United States.

• They have been willing to limit, and sometimes to eliminate altogether, weapon programs that encountered technical problems or otherwise did not meet their expectations (e.g., the Galosh ABM system, the SS-16 mobile ICBM, the Typhoon missile-carrying submarine, the co-orbital ASAT interceptor).

• They have been prepared to accept limitations in areas in which the United States was likely to have a technological edge (e.g., ALCMs).

• They have been willing to dismantle or destroy aging systems or systems that had reached the end of their useful lifetimes (e.g., SS-7s and SS-8s in SALT I, SS-4s in INF, and a reduction to 2,250 strategic delivery vehicles in SALT II involving the retirement mostly of SS-11 ICBMs and aging bombers).

• They have also been prepared to accept limitations where the specific levels set were consistent with or not very far from planned levels (e.g., a 2,400 delivery vehicle aggregate in SALT II and a freeze on ballistic missile launchers in SALT I).

Soviet Inflexibility and the Limits of U.S. Leverage

The Soviet approach to arms control bears little resemblance to the flexible bargaining characteristic of a Middle Eastern bazaar where merchants are prepared, even eager, to trade away anything in their diverse inventories as long as the price is right. The Soviet weapon inventory is hardly up for grabs. Some systems the Soviets are prepared to give up for a suitable price. Others, especially those needed to achieve critical military objectives, will either be much more expensive or simply not for sale. And unlike the free-wheeling negotiating environment of the bazaar, the Soviet military planning system imposes a framework of rigidity and caution.

A sovereign state, especially a military superpower, will accept an arms control agreement only if it calculates that the agreement will leave it better off—or at least no worse off—than it would be in the absence of mutual constraints. And in making such a calculation, that sovereign power will naturally be guided by its own national objectives, its own perceptions of equity and balance, and its own assessment of the forces it requires to achieve its objectives. A key obstacle the United States has encountered in pursuing its arms control negotiating goals is that the Soviet arms it has tried hardest to limit are precisely the ones that rank highest in the Soviet hierarchy of military requirements. The Soviets have often made the judgment that they would be better off holding onto their highly-prized military assets than accepting an agreement that would trade away those assets in exchange for limits on the United States.

4

Nonmilitary Influences on
Soviet Negotiating Behavior

In trying to predict or evaluate Soviet positions in arms control negotiations, there is a tendency among Western analysts to assume that Soviet negotiating behavior is guided by military considerations — by narrow, technical assessments of the military trade-offs involved in limiting U.S. and Soviet defense programs. In many respects, of course, this focus on the military dimension is justified. The Soviets can be counted upon to weigh the military implications of any possible agreement very carefully and to sign it only if, at a minimum, it does not adversely affect Soviet security.

But factors outside the military realm — foreign policy goals, internal considerations, economic incentives, and so forth — also have a major impact on Soviet arms control decision making, encouraging the Soviet government to move toward or away from agreement. Indeed, especially in cases in which the military impact of an agreement is minimal, nonmilitary considerations will often provide the principal explanation for Soviet behavior at the negotiating table. The influential role of these nonmilitary factors is another reason — aside from the relatively weak incentives the Soviets often have to constrain U.S. defense programs and from the strong reluctance they often have to constrain their own — why U.S. negotiating leverage is frequently both limited and hard to predict.

Integral Role of Nonmilitary Factors

In the Soviet Union, nonmilitary considerations appear to influence arms control behavior more than in the United States. In general, the United States regards arms control as essentially a technical exercise in military force architecture. By altering numerical levels and qualitative characteristics, the United States seeks to remodel the force structure of both sides to strengthen stability and promote U.S. security interests. This is not to suggest that foreign policy and domestic considerations have no effect on U.S. arms control behavior. Clearly they do, and at some times more than others — such as in efforts to practice "linkage," and in presidential election years. But the main thrust of U.S. arms control policy has been to serve military-strategic objectives, and this emphasis has most often dominated U.S. negotiating proposals over the years.

The Soviets clearly have not viewed arms control as a narrow, technical device to achieve isolated military goals. Instead, they have treated it as an integral part of a broad foreign and defense policy in which all the elements are intended to be mutually reinforcing and in which the nonmilitary objectives of arms control can be just as important as the strictly military ones.

One reason that Soviet arms control policy serves political, economic, and other Soviet objectives as well as security interests can be found in the Soviet approach to evaluating national power and influence. The Soviet concept of "the correlation of forces" takes into account not only the static and operational dimensions of each side's military forces but also a wide range of less tangible, nonmilitary components of national power, including "political and economic strength, alliance support, leadership quality, and national resolve."[24] Accordingly, arms control proposals or agreements that elevate the USSR's international standing, weaken NATO's coherence, inhibit improvement in Sino-U.S. relations, or undermine U.S. public support for defense efforts may be seen by Soviet leaders as just as valuable as agreements that bring benefits in the more tangible military indicators of national strength.

Another reason for the prominence of nonmilitary factors in Soviet decision making is that the Soviets, having relied relatively little on arms control to solve critical security problems, can afford militarily to use arms control as an instrument to promote a wide variety of nonmilitary objectives. Thus, in addition to pursuing militarily significant agreements whenever such measures might promote Soviet security interests, the Soviets also have the latitude to negotiate agreements that are essentially cosmetic from a military standpoint in order to further other goals. On occasions in which progress in negotiations would not suit overall Soviet needs, they can afford from a military perspective to delay or block agreement. Thus, given the already sizeable Soviet advantage in INF systems, their "hot" SS-20 production line, and their ability to deploy new, shorter range INF missiles in Eastern Europe, the Soviets had the "luxury" of being able to walk out of the INF negotiations in order to demonstrate their displeasure with the Reagan administration's policies, to stimulate discord within NATO, and to shake Western resolve to continue with Pershing and GLCM deployments.

Foreign Policy Motivations

Perceived foreign policy benefits have provided strong incentives for the Soviets to move toward arms control agreements. Those incentives were probably strongest in the case of SALT I, in which the primary Soviet military objective of constraining U.S. ABM capabilities was supplemented by a range of powerful foreign policy interests.

One of the least tangible but most important of those interests was to bolster Soviet international standing and prestige. Having invested massive resources to build up their strategic nuclear capabilities, the Soviets wanted an agreement that would codify their status as a superpower and ensure for them the political benefits that might be expected to flow from their international recognition as an equal, at least militarily, of the leader of the capitalist camp.

Soviet leaders probably believed that the formalization of parity in SALT I would have other profound geopolitical effects. They may well have hoped that it would persuade Americans once and for all to abandon what the Soviets consider to be the U.S. goal of military superiority and the U.S. expectation that it would call the tune for the Soviet Union on the international stage. In a related manner, Soviet leaders may have thought that codification of parity would affect West European attitudes, particularly that it could undermine the confidence of European NATO members in the reliability of U.S. security guarantees and lead, over time, to a loosening of transatlantic ties.

The Soviets probably also calculated that progress on SALT could help them nail down one of their key foreign policy objectives of the postwar period — the recognition and consolidation of the status quo in Europe as embodied in West Germany's Eastern treaties and in the four-power agreement on Berlin. The U.S.-USSR SALT talks tended to encourage and legitimize the Federal Republic's *Ostpolitik* by leaving the Bonn government less isolated in its dealing with the East. Moreover, the Soviets probably saw the pace of those European détente negotiations tied to progress in SALT and indeed may well have figured that the Bundestag's ratification of the Eastern treaties would be facilitated by tangible progress in the East-West military negotiations.[25]

Another important foreign policy incentive for the Soviets in SALT I was to inhibit the growing rapprochement between the United States and China. Among the events that stimulated Soviet interest in reaching an early arms control accord were the revelation of Henry Kissinger's secret 1971 visit to Beijing and President Nixon's visit to China in February 1972. The Soviets believed, according to an observer of the negotiations, that "a SALT agreement would put China's role and Chinese pretensions in perspective as nothing else could" and would show the Chinese that "the major business on the East-West agenda could only be performed by the superpowers."[26] Given these Soviet incentives, the Nixon administration's opening to China is widely credited with encouraging greater Soviet flexibility in the latter stages of SALT I.

Although the foreign policy motivations for Soviet movement in arms control have perhaps been most evident in SALT I, they also played a role in other arms control negotiations. The Limited Test Ban Treaty of 1963, which followed several months after President John F. Kennedy's conciliatory American University speech, can be understood more as a purposeful step toward détente than as a meaningful constraint on U.S.-Soviet military competition. Incidentally, it is interesting, considering the subsequent SALT experience with triangular diplomacy, that the successful Limited Test Ban Treaty negotiations in Moscow followed a breakdown in Sino-Soviet discussions and the opening of a Sino-U.S. channel of communications in Warsaw.

The Vladivostok accord of SALT II in November 1974, in which the Soviets agreed for the first time to a key U.S. demand for equal aggregates in strategic delivery vehicles, can probably be attributed as much to foreign policy motives (the Soviet desire to give a boost to a sagging détente and to get off on the right foot with the recently elevated President Gerald Ford) as to strictly military considerations (e.g., U.S. willingness to accept fairly high levels of delivery vehicles).

During the 1970s the United States and Soviet Union negotiated several arms control agreements that had minor or even negligible military effects but that the Soviets were interested in concluding for a variety of foreign policy and other reasons. From the Soviet perspective, neither the 1971 Seabeds Treaty nor the 1972 Biological Weapons Convention was seen as having any practical military effect on the United States, which had no plans to emplace nuclear weapons on the ocean floor and had years earlier unilaterally destroyed its own biological weapons. Nonetheless, Soviet leaders presumably saw political advantage in taking a leading role, together with the United States, in achieving multilateral arms control agreements, thereby bolstering the Soviet image, both at home and abroad, as a champion of peace and a constructive player on the world stage.

Similarly, despite the fact that the U.S. Congress had refused the Nixon administration the funds to construct the second ABM complex permitted under the 1972 ABM Treaty, the Soviets agreed in 1974 to the ABM Treaty Protocol, reducing the number of permitted complexes from two to one. Even though the Soviet Union had traditionally relied on high-yield nuclear weapons testing more than had the United States, the Soviets agreed to the 150-kiloton Threshold Test Ban Treaty in 1974, recognizing that the military effects on the United States would be marginal, perhaps even less than on themselves. Both agreements were concluded at the 1974 "Watergate summit" in Moscow and were probably viewed by Brezhnev and the other Soviet leaders as giving additional support to the structure of détente and perhaps also as lending a helping hand to their teetering negotiating partner, Richard Nixon.

Soviet foreign policy considerations have also worked against more accommodating positions in arms control negotiations. In late 1978, for example, the Soviets reacted to the U.S. initiative to normalize relations with China by digging in their heels and slowing the completion of SALT II, thus sending a message of dissatisfaction while waiting to see the results of the U.S. visit by Chinese leader Deng Xiaoping in early 1979.

Ever since the bilateral INF negotiations began in the fall of 1980 and then resumed in late 1981 under the Reagan administration, the Soviets may well have calculated that, from the standpoint of Soviet foreign policy objectives, they were better off *not* achieving agreement, except on their own terms – which called for no U.S. INF missile deployment. In the absence of an agreement, they may have reasoned, the INF issue would be a constant irritant within the Western alliance, especially given the drawn out schedule of deployments. At a minimum, this would provide opportunities for the Soviets to try to increase friction between the United States and its allies as well as to stimulate antinuclear, anti-

NATO, and anti-American sentiment within West European societies, particularly in the major opposition parties. At best, this divisive situation might result in decisions by Western governments not to proceed with the deployments, thus enabling the Soviets to secure their objective without paying the price of reducing their own missiles.

By contrast, an agreement that permitted the deployment of U.S. missiles (albeit at a reduced level) would have several unattractive features from the Soviet perspective. In particular, it would tend to restore unity within NATO and would thus reduce Soviet opportunities to play on internal divisions. And by "legitimizing" U.S. deployments, the Soviets would also concede defeat in their attempt to reverse a major Western security initiative.

An agreement would, of course, bring some compensating foreign policy benefits, including an improvement in Soviet-West European relations, which had been strained by the INF affair, and the alleviation of East European concerns about the deterioration of East-West relations and about Soviet "counterdeployments" on their territory. But these benefits, at least so far, seem to have been outweighed by the foreign policy costs of reaching an agreement as well as by the military calculation that the kind of agreement the West appears insistent upon would leave the Soviets worse off than they would be if INF systems remained unconstrained.

Recently, foreign policy considerations have had a major, and almost exclusively negative, impact on Soviet arms control behavior. Throughout 1984, the Soviets kept arms control essentially in the deep freeze to dramatize their displeasure with the overall thrust of U.S. policy toward the USSR, to sow divisions within the Western alliance, and to avoid doing anything to help the reelection of President Reagan. Although the Soviets would clearly have objected to certain elements of U.S. arms control positions regardless of the state of bilateral relations, they apparently decided, for political reasons, to put the worst possible face on all U.S. initiatives during 1984, taking a high-handed, dismissive approach toward proposals they might otherwise have chosen to explore more carefully, including the April 1984 NATO proposal in MBFR, the announced U.S. willingness to consider a nonuse of force pledge in the context of confidence-building measures for Europe, and signs of U.S. flexibility in START in late 1983.

State of U.S.-Soviet Relations

In charting the ebb and flow of the U.S.-Soviet relationship over the last 15 years, one finds a strong correlation between periods of improving bilateral relations and periods of progress in arms control. Part of the explanation for this undoubtedly lies on the U.S. side of the equation. But a substantial part can also be attributed to the Soviet belief that arms control is not an isolated, technical phenomenon but an integral element of an overall foreign and defense policy whose various components should reinforce one another.

At times when the bilateral relationship has been relatively positive or on the upswing, the Soviets have seen advantage in concluding arms control agreements as a means of further strengthening the relationship and of achieving the gains they have regarded as flowing from improved relations, such as relaxation of tensions and greater access to Western goods, technology, and credits. In these circumstances, the Soviets have had incentives to be more flexible in arms control negotiations. This greater flexibility is likely to result both from a conscious, purposeful effort to reinforce positive trends in bilateral relations and from the internal facts of Soviet life. Internally, Soviet leaders find it much easier to marshall the necessary support for difficult negotiating concessions if those concessions can be justified as serving broad foreign policy goals, not just as obtaining a narrow technical quid pro quo. Moreover, an improving U.S.-Soviet relationship will create greater receptivity in the Politburo for limiting Soviet defense capabilities (in exchange, of course, for suitable limits on U.S. programs) than will a relationship characterized by high levels of tension, mistrust, and military competition.

When the state of bilateral relations is worsening or is already bad, the Soviets have much less incentive to move ahead in arms control. An isolated arms control measure concluded in a political vacuum with little prospect of bringing wider political benefits has relatively little appeal. And the necessary bureaucratic support will be hard to muster when the bilateral relationship is an antagonistic one. This is not to suggest that, when relations are bad, the Soviets will reject arms control agreements that would be militarily advantageous to them. Regardless of the state of relations, the Soviets will be interested in measures that serve their security interests. But they will be less willing and able to make significant concessions to obtain such measures, and, as a practical matter, this will dampen prospects for meaningful arms control.

This point is illustrated by the strange ambivalence with which the Soviet government approached its own proposal in June 1984 to begin negotiations on space weapons the following September in Vienna. Clearly the Soviets are concerned by U.S. space-related weapon programs and would like to see them stopped. So, despite the bad state of U.S.-Soviet relations and the Soviet interest in not aiding President Reagan's reelection, the Soviets proposed the space talks, probably expecting the United States to turn them down. The Reagan administration's answer that it was willing to discuss space weapons (while making clear that it also planned to raise the question of offensive forces) put the Soviets on the defensive. But, given their interest in blocking U.S. space programs, they probably still would have gone ahead with the talks if the United States had been prepared to participate on their terms: a moratorium on testing and an agenda restricted to space weapons. When it became clear that Washington was not prepared to play by their rather prejudicial rules – and that any restrictions on space systems, if negotiable at all, would not come cheap – the Soviets decided to drop the matter for the time being. In a more positive climate of bilateral relations, the outcome would almost surely have been different.

Domestic Factors

Just as foreign policy objectives may prompt greater Soviet flexibility in arms control, so may internal political considerations provide incentives for Soviet movement toward agreement. For example, international agreements, particularly arms control agreements with the United States, can boost the standing of the Soviet leader and his supporters within the Kremlin and help them consolidate or increase their power. And although public opinion obviously plays a different and much more limited role in the USSR than in the United States, there is a sense in which arms control agreements can enable the Soviet leadership to bolster its own legitimacy and public support by seeming to respond to the Soviet citizens' desire for peace and to their hope that there is a limit to the sacrifices they will be required to make for national defense. Just as U.S. presidents may sometimes see domestic political advantage in signing arms control agreements at summit conferences, so may their Soviet counterparts have domestic incentives to play a highly visible role as peacemaker.

Domestic factors can also inhibit Soviet flexibility in arms control, however. Any arms control agreement involving substantial constraints on Soviet military capabilities is likely to face resistance from segments of the Soviet ruling circle, particularly the military. During the past two decades the Soviet military and defense industries have acquired extraordinary influence in the allocation of Soviet economic resources and have used that influence to ensure their claims would be given priority. The military has also exercised considerable authority in the Soviet arms control decision-making process.

Given the institutional clout of those in Moscow who are most reluctant to constrain Soviet capabilities, it has taken a strong Kremlin leader to push through the Politburo the concessions necessary to seal an agreement with the United States. In this regard, it is believed that Brezhnev greatly consolidated his internal position in March 1971 at the twenty-fourth Communist Party congress – appointing four supporters to the Politburo and assuming increased control over economic policies – and that his strengthened position enabled him to negotiate the key SALT I breakthrough in May of that year and to conclude the accords one year later. Indeed, without Brezhnev clearly in charge, it would have been difficult to imagine the Soviets making several of the key arms control concessions of the mid-1970s, including the exclusion of U.S. forward-based aircraft from SALT (reportedly over the strong opposition of the General Staff), the moratorium on peaceful nuclear explosions and the agreement to allow 10 seismic stations on Soviet territory in the comprehensive test ban negotiations (presumably over the opposition, respectively, of the atomic energy bureaucracy and the internal security apparatus).

Over the last several years, the extended period of transition in the Soviet leadership has made prospects for productive arms control negotiations even more remote than they might otherwise have been. Former Under Secretary of State Lawrence S. Eagleburger spoke in March 1984 about the implications of dealing with three different Soviet leaders within a three-year period:

> This substantial period of succession politics, in my opinion, has had a major impact on the ability of the Soviet Union to make decisions. Productive negotiations require flexibility, and flexibility requires leadership that is willing to make difficult decisions and accept responsibility for them. The Soviet Union has not had such leadership during the Reagan Administration. Virtually without exception, each time the Soviets have been faced with difficult choices we have witnessed a period of apparent internal debate followed, inevitably, by hard-line decisions clearly dictated by the most conservative elements in the Politburo.[27]

Another internal factor inhibiting the ability of Soviet negotiators to respond flexibly to changing proposals and incentives is the rigid nature of the Soviet decision-making process. Decisions on key arms control issues are usually taken at the senior-most level, sometimes in the face of intense bureaucratic rivalry. Once a controversial issue is resolved, there is strong reluctance to revisit it. Although the decision may lay down a general line of policy with considerable room for tactical maneuver in negotiations, the line itself will be difficult to alter.

Thus, in addition to the Soviets' other reasons for rejecting the U.S. March 1977 proposal in SALT II (e.g., its alleged one-sidedness and the public manner in which it was presented), the Soviets have emphasized that it was a radical departure from the Vladivostok framework to which Brezhnev had committed his prestige and for which, he claimed, he had to shed blood at home.

Similarly, given the way the Soviet bureaucracy works, it is not surprising that the Soviet position in START is essentially an updated version of the SALT II Treaty signed at the 1979 Vienna summit. Although several of the ceilings are lower, such as the 1,800 limit on delivery vehicles compared to 2,250, the differences can be explained by timing, not a basic change in policy. Although START II required reductions from 2,500 to 2,250 between June 1979 and January 1981, the Soviet START proposal would not require the 1,800 level to be reached before 1990 (and the reductions could be taken largely in older ICBMs and SLBMs). Thus, the START proposal was precisely the type of conservative decision that could be taken by a bureaucracy accustomed to incremental change, especially at a time of flux in the Kremlin leadership.

Economic Incentives

Reducing the burden of defense spending on the economy is among the most powerful incentives the Soviet government might be expected to have for pursuing arms control. Since the beginning of the Brezhnev era, that burden has been substantial. Defense expenditures, according to the U.S. Central Intelligence Agency, grew at an average rate of 4–5 percent in real terms between 1965 and 1980 and by 1980 accounted for between 12 and 14 percent of the gross national product (more than double the burden in the United States and Britain). Moreover, the defense sector has had first call on equipment, material, and personnel and has deprived the civilian economy of its potentially most productive resources.[28]

Although it is logical that freeing up economic resources from the defense sector would be on the minds of Soviet leaders as they approach arms control, there is little evidence that economic pressures, at least so far, have had a significant impact on Soviet negotiating behavior. It is true that the Soviets probably believed in the early 1970s that arms control agreements, by contributing to an overall improvement in bilateral relations, could yield some indirect economic benefits, such as greater Soviet access to Western goods, technology, and credits. And certain Soviet arms control proposals, such as the proposal to ban cruise missiles, may have been driven in part by the desire to avoid an expensive competition in arms and other countermeasures. But the Soviets have not exhibited much of an inclination to alter their military requirements or negotiating priorities in the face of such economic considerations. Their desire to hold down spending on air defenses, for example, was apparently not strong enough to induce them to consider the kind of substantial changes in their own force plans that would have been required to interest the United States in a cruise missile ban.

In the future, however, Soviet resource allocation problems are expected to become much more acute. The rate of Soviet economic growth has been declining steadily since the late 1960s, when the average annual growth in GNP was more than 5 percent. Western analysts believe that growth over the next decade will be in the neighborhood of 2 percent.[29] When overall economic growth was relatively high, the Soviets could afford to fund their substantial defense buildup and still permit increases in the rate of civil investment and consumption. Indeed, since 1965 the Soviet consumer's standard of living has improved considerably.[30] But as the overall economic growth rate has slowed (and been outstripped by the rate of growth of military spending), the Soviet leadership has increasingly been faced with hard choices. As one U.S. expert has written:

> If the Soviets must continue to increase military spending as fast or faster than it did in the last decade, this would produce stagnation or even decline in consumer spending, and would cut into investments in the Soviet economy that are crucial to modernize and increase labor productivity. . . . So, for the first time in the post-Stalin years, the growth of Soviet military spending has become an insurmountable barrier to increasing consumer spending and investment in agriculture and industry.[31]

It is clear, therefore, that in the future the Soviets will be under great pressure to find ways to hold down defense spending. But it is not at all clear that the pessimistic economic outlook for the Soviet Union will have a decisive, or even major, impact on Soviet behavior in arms control.

In the first place, the institutional pressures to sustain a high level of defense spending may be just as great or greater than the pressures to shift resources to the civilian economy. The defense establishment's claims on economic resources are firmly entrenched. But, more important, military spending does not constitute a "special interest" in the Soviet Union. Party and military elites have been united on the overriding importance of military power in promoting Soviet national interests and on its paramount position in Soviet economic priorities.

Even if there were broad support for cutting back military spending, the areas of defense that might provide the best opportunities for savings, such as conventional arms procurement and manpower, would probably not be affected by arms control. In this connection, the Soviet Strategic Rocket Forces, which are the heart of the Soviet nuclear deterrent and the central focus of U.S. attention at the bargaining table, are believed to account only for about 9 percent of the Soviet military outlay.[32]

Moreover, arms control agreements involving only marginal adjustments of existing force levels – of the type we have seen so far in the area of strategic offensive arms – hold out little prospect of significant economic savings and thus have little attraction to the Soviets from a strictly economic point of view. And far-reaching arms control proposals such as the 1982 U.S. START offer may well involve strong economic disincentives for the USSR if they would require a costly restructuring of Soviet capabilities.

For the Soviets, the main economic incentives for arms control come not from the possibility of reducing existing forces but from the possibility of avoiding new and expensive areas of competition. They will have an increasingly strong economic interest in preventing the United States from pursuing the types of programs that might require them to make rapid, large-scale changes in their force structure, such as advanced ballistic missile defenses. Accordingly, they may be more inclined than previously to make significant negotiating concessions to head off those U.S. programs.

But it is easy to exaggerate the extent to which the Soviet Union's growing economic predicament will enable the United States to dictate the terms of future arms control agreements. The Soviets would face tough choices, but the choice would still be theirs – and they could always elect to rob from immediate consumer demands and long-term civil investment needs to pay for an arms race with the United States. Such a choice would not be without profound costs. Although lowering of the Soviet standard of living, for example, would not be likely to lead to unmanageable social unrest, it could result in much more widespread disillusionment and dissatisfaction with the Soviet system, which in turn would have negative implications for future economic performance and the legitimacy of the system. But if the alternative were an arms control agreement forcing the Soviets to accept what they considered to be a position of inferiority, the Soviet leadership would most likely choose competition and sacrifice.

In addition, although a massive U.S. arms buildup could put the Soviets under great stress and perhaps win some important concessions at the negotiating table, U.S. leaders should be under no illusions about the readiness of the United States as a society to mount a challenge of the magnitude that would be required. The U.S. economy is undoubtedly stronger than that of the Soviet Union. But public pressures to hold down military spending are also undoubtedly stronger than in the Soviet Union. Indeed, in an all-out arms race, the U.S. threshold of pain may well be lower.

Perceptions of U.S. Resolve, Coherence, and Consistency

In addition to foreign policy goals, internal incentives and constraints, and economic influences, Soviet negotiating behavior can be affected by nonmilitary considerations of an even less tangible character. In particular, Moscow's willingness to make concessions in arms control negotiations can be influenced by its perceptions of the will, internal unity, flexibility, and steadiness of its principal adversary and negotiating partner, the United States.

As an example, Soviet flexibility might be increased by the perception that the United States would be prepared to forgo an agreement if an agreement could not be reached on terms the United States considered acceptable. To create such a perception the United States would need not only to have in train the programs necessary to support its military requirements in the absence of arms control, but also be able to convey the impression that it was prepared, if its negotiating objectives were not achieved, to walk away from the negotiating table and implement those programs fully – and to absorb whatever political costs might be associated with such actions. If the Soviets believe the United States "needs" arms control, either militarily or politically, they will consider themselves in a much better position to hold out for their terms.

Demonstrating the resolve to make do, if necessary, without an agreement, however, does not mean projecting the image that the United States would *prefer* to live without one. If Soviet leaders should gain the impression, through initial U.S. proposals and subsequent negotiating behavior, that the United States is not interested in reaching agreement, they will have little incentive to push internally for the hard Soviet concessions required to close a deal. In its statements and actions, the United States should make clear that it is determined, one way or the other, to meet its security requirements—preferably at lower cost and risk through arms control but alternatively, if a satisfactory agreement cannot be achieved, through unilateral efforts.

Soviet incentives to negotiate flexibly may also be influenced by perceptions of the domestic political strength of the U.S. president. On the one hand, a strong president will increase those incentives because he will be seen by the Soviets as capable both of obtaining domestic support for his defense programs and of overcoming the internal obstacles to making the U.S. concessions necessary to achieve agreement. On the other hand, the Soviets may well become more rigid at the negotiating table if they see a U.S. president unable to achieve sufficient discipline within his own administration or sufficient support from the Congress and the U.S. public to pursue a coherent, purposeful approach either to arms control or to defense programs. Such a perception could convince the Soviets that any further concessions on their part would simply go unreciprocated and not lead to agreement.

In this connection, Soviet doubts about the political strength and staying power of Richard Nixon after the Watergate affair began to weaken his presidency contributed to the lack of progress in SALT between 1973 and mid-1974. That stage of negotiations was marked by deep and publicly evident divisions over SALT policy within the administration, persistent attacks on the administration's approach to SALT by congressional critics, and ineffective leadership by an increasingly distracted and debilitated president. In these circumstances, the Soviets were content to bide their time.

As Henry Kissinger has written, "The likelihood that the Nixon Presidency was coming to an early end must certainly have affected the Politburo's calculations about how many more concessions were sensible in this round of negotiations."[33]

Similarly, Soviet reluctance in 1979 and 1980 to make further concessions in the trilateral comprehensive test ban negotiations can be attributed to some extent to serious doubts in Moscow that President Carter would be able to bring the talks to a successful conclusion in the face of determined opposition by certain parts of his administration. In 1978 and 1979 the Soviets had seen the president make a number of significant changes in the U.S. negotiating position in response to pressures from domestic test ban opponents, such as the shift from a treaty of unlimited duration, to a five-year treaty, then a three-year treaty. Faced with the possibility that President Carter might not be able to deliver his own bureaucracy, the Soviets, who had made most of the significant concessions so far in the negotiations, began to harden their position and the talks soon became deadlocked.

Sometimes Soviet negotiating incentives may be affected not just by perceptions of domestic support for the U.S. president, but also by perceptions of domestic support for individual U.S. defense programs. In this regard, the relative ease with which successive administrations have been able to secure congressional approval of appropriations for the ALCM program has presumably reinforced existing Soviet concerns about ALCMs and increased Soviet incentives for placing constraints on them. The affirmative congressional actions have demonstrated not only that existing programmatic goals are likely to be met but, perhaps more important from the standpoint of negotiating leverage, that the program may be expanded in the future.

By the same token, it might be assumed that Soviet negotiating incentives would decrease as a result of weak or heavily qualified congressional or public support for a U.S. program. This assumption is frequently reflected in arguments, advanced most often before key congressional votes on the defense budget, that failure to approve the full administration requests for certain programs will adversely affect prospects for negotiations. Clearly, there is merit in such arguments. If the Soviets believe that a program will be killed in Congress, they will hardly be inclined to pay much of a price to constrain it by agreement. But in practice, the extent to which weak or wavering domestic support will actually convince the Soviets that a program is no longer a threat — and will therefore make them less interested in placing constraints on it — is probably overdrawn.

In assessing the impact of our domestic defense debate on our eventual force posture, the Soviets probably make what from their perspective are worst-case assumptions. And looking at the record of U.S. defense procurement, such assumptions would most often be justified. A substantial number of U.S. programs have been controversial, several have been delayed or stretched out, and some, such as the B-1, even temporarily canceled. But rarely has the Congress managed to kill a major weapons program or even to scale back significantly the number of units eventually deployed.

Moreover, the Soviets recognize that, even if the Congress were to hobble or defer a U.S. program on the assumption that there was no Soviet counterpart or that its counterpart was inactive or ineffective, there would be strong pressures on the Congress to resume the U.S. program if Soviet efforts in that area were to pick up in the future. The Safeguard ABM program provides an example of this. After approving the administration's requests for Phase I of Safeguard, congressional support for the program dropped off sharply. It was clear to the Soviets by 1971 that four, at most, of the program's original 12 sites would be built and that the nationwide defense they feared was not politically feasible in the United States. Yet instead of relying on continued U.S. domestic opposition to achieve their objective, the Soviets continued to negotiate seriously in SALT I and eventually to conclude the ABM Treaty. Presumably the Soviets understood that, if they proceeded with their own ABM program, the Congress would have no choice but to authorize the resumption of Safeguard. Similarly, the Soviets must recognize that, despite current sentiment in parts of Congress for delaying the U.S. ASAT program, this sentiment would evaporate quickly if they were to show forward movement in their own ASAT efforts.

Thus, although the Soviets put a great deal of effort into influencing the U.S. defense debate, they will be reluctant to count on domestic U.S. pressures to place permanent constraints on U.S. programs of concern to them. Weak or wavering domestic support for a U.S. program will often reduce the urgency the Soviets attach to arms control, but it will not, in many cases, significantly reduce their incentives for achieving negotiated constraints. In general, Soviet incentives to limit a particular U.S. program will be determined much more by the Soviet Union's original assessment of the program's implications than by the day-to-day perturbations of the complex and volatile U.S. defense procurement process.

The Emotional Dimension

Soviet negotiating behavior is usually assumed to be a rational, calculating effort to maximize various national, organizational, or even personal interests — whether those interests take the form of security benefits, foreign policy goals, internal power and legitimacy, alleviation of economic strains, and so on. But cool rationality does not always govern Soviet arms control behavior, just as it does not always govern such behavior in the United States. There is a strong human, emotional dimension that can impinge on the process.

The emotional content of negative Soviet actions in arms control in recent years should not be underestimated. The Soviet walkout from the INF negotiations in November 1983, for example, cannot be explained strictly in calm, interest-maximizing terms. To be sure, there were some calculating elements in the Soviet temper tantrum. They wanted to raise the temperature level in East-West relations in the hope of persuading West European host governments to rethink the deployments and in the expectation, at a minimum, of creating friction between the United States and its allies. They also believed – having made the claim publicly and at the highest levels that a military balance existed before Western missile deployments – they had to restore the balance through counterdeployments before resuming talks. But the Soviets have probably let certain U.S. actions get under their skin. Comments by some U.S. officials, for instance, that the Soviets would not negotiate seriously until the missile deployments got under way in late 1983 rankled them and may well have guaranteed that they would not negotiate at all once the deployments got under way.

Similarly, the Soviets are extremely sensitive to the appearance of knuckling in to U.S. pressures. Having built up its huge military arsenal in part to avoid having to fear coercion by the United States, the USSR bristles at the implication that the United States might be able to call the shots in arms control negotiations as a result of a U.S. military buildup. As former Soviet leader Yuri Andropov mentioned in a Pravda interview:

> The American leadership, as all signs indicate, has not given up its intentions to conduct talks with us from positions of strength, from positions of threats and pressure. We resolutely reject such an approach. And, in general, attempts to conduct a "power diplomacy" in respect of us are a hopeless thing.[34]

Soviet responses to U.S. arms control initiatives in recent years can certainly be explained by a variety of motivations other than human emotion. But the strong and emotional desire not to vindicate the Reagan policy of "negotiating from strength" was a contributing factor.

The Impact of Nonmilitary Factors

Despite the influential role that foreign policy, domestic, economic, and other nonmilitary considerations have played in Soviet arms control decision making, these nonmilitary incentives alone have not been sufficient to induce the Soviets to accept significant limits on their military capabilities. The historical record seems to indicate that in every instance in which the Soviets were prepared to accept substantial constraints on their military strength, the benefits they required as compensation were, at least in part, constraints on U.S. military capabilities.

Nonetheless, factors outside the military realm have had a major impact on the arms control process over the past 15 years. In the case of SALT I, critical foreign policy objectives combined with Soviet interest in limiting U.S. ABM potential to produce Soviet acceptance of the first major bilateral arms control agreement. In cases where the military effects were relatively minor or cosmetic, nonmilitary considerations played the decisive role in bringing the Soviets along. Moreover, even in agreements in which military factors tended to provide the chief motivation and to determine the substantive outcome, foreign policy or internal pressures often determined their timing — and indeed whether the agreements would be concluded at all.

Thus U.S. defense programs may often provide the necessary condition for arms control agreements. Without the opportunity to limit those programs, the Soviets would find little incentive to accept constraints on their own military capabilities. But U.S. programs alone will rarely, if ever, provide the sufficient conditions. The sufficient conditions will often involve a range of foreign policy, domestic, economic, and even less tangible considerations.

In view of the importance of these nonmilitary incentives and constraints in Soviet negotiating behavior, it is worth considering whether the United States can manipulate them to promote its own negotiating objectives. The Soviets, after all, routinely seek — although with less success than they are often credited with — to influence U.S. arms control behavior by attempting to generate pressures from U.S. allies, to influence U.S. public opinion, and to affect the U.S. military planning and budgeting process.

But the opportunities for influence are not symmetrical. Most of the Soviet opportunities depend on the openness and democratic character of the U.S. political system. Comparable opportunities to influence the internal debate in the Soviet Union—such as it is—simply do not exist. Indeed, we know virtually nothing about that debate and probably could do little to affect it even if we did.

From time to time, the United States may see targets of opportunity such as upcoming summit conferences or Communist Party congresses, in which, according to U.S. estimates, a Kremlin leader has strong incentives to show progress in arms control and therefore to adopt more flexible positions in negotiations. Such precipitating events may indeed prompt greater Soviet flexibility. But they are likely simply to accelerate the pace of negotiations rather than alter their substantive outcome in major ways. Moreover, such targets of opportunity only arise infrequently and, in some cases such as with summits, the pressures for concessions will cut both ways.

In principle, it is possible to use rewards or penalties in the areas of foreign policy and economics to obtain Soviet concessions in arms control negotiations. Henry Kissinger sought, perhaps with some success, to manipulate Soviet incentives in this way. For example, recognizing Soviet eagerness to nail down the Berlin agreement and the Eastern treaties, Kissinger reports that he tacitly linked the pace of these negotiations to the SALT talks to induce Soviet flexibility on the latter.[35]

Such specific, tactical linkages may sometimes work, but they will not always be available, politically feasible, or consistent with other U.S. objectives. It requires both that the Soviets want something from us (e.g., codification of the status quo in Europe) and that the United States (perhaps together with its allies) be prepared, in exchange for Soviet flexibility in arms control, to satisfy that desire. But how often will such conditions be met, especially at a time of bad U.S.-Soviet relations? There may be all sorts of political and economic "carrots" that would be appealing to the Soviets (such as a Soviet role in a formal Middle East peacemaking process, the suspension of U.S. support for rebels in Afghanistan, and the easing of restrictions on trade and technology transfer). But such carrots will often be inconsistent with other U.S. policy goals.

Specific political and economic "sticks" would be even harder to use than carrots as a means of achieving particular Soviet arms control concessions. As the U.S. experience since Afghanistan has demonstrated, sanctions may be useful as a means of making a political statement or as a means of punishment, but they hardly ever succeed in persuading the victim of sanctions to modify his behavior.

Political and economic benefits are less likely to provide incentives for more flexible Soviet negotiating behavior if they are dangled in front of the Soviets as isolated, tactical quids pro quo than if they are part of an overall improvement in bilateral relations. In the context of improving relations, the Soviets are likely to believe that movement in arms control would serve broader goals and therefore be more advantageous. But even in the context of substantially improved bilateral relations, the Soviets will not be inclined to accept limitations on their military capabilities that they consider inequitable or that they believe will undercut their ability to achieve important military requirements.

5

Current Controversies

Over the past 15 years of more-or-less active arms control negotiations, there have been recurring debates over the impact of U.S. weapon programs on Soviet negotiating behavior. The programs have changed, but the arguments have remained remarkably the same. Drawing on the preceding analysis, this chapter seeks to shed light on some of the latest versions of these current controversies. In particular, it will address the implications for U.S. negotiating leverage of two controversial U.S. weapons programs—binary chemical weapons and the MX ICBM.

Binary Chemical Weapons and Arms Control

One of the most controversial items in each year's defense budget debate, and the one major weapons program in which the Reagan administration has had little success with the Congress, has been the binary CW program. All funds requested for the binary program were deleted from the fiscal year 1985 defense bill—as they had been the previous several years—thus ensuring a continuation of the 15-year hiatus in the production of U.S. chemical weapons that began in 1969.[36]

Given heightened public and congressional interest in arms control in recent years, it was inevitable that arguments about the impact of the binary program on prospects for on-going CW arms control negotiations would play a prominent role in the budgetary debates. Thus, on the eve of the 1984 House vote on the administration's binary request, President Reagan wrote: "This modest offensive modernization effort is needed to keep the pressure on the Soviet Union to nego-tiate a meaningful agreement."[37] Opponents argued that pro-duction of binaries would stimulate further Soviet efforts in the CW area and decrease prospects for productive negotia-tions. On the House floor, for example, Congressman Berkley Bedell maintained that

> the approval of this funding request will undermine present U.S. arms control efforts that are aimed at the achievement of a chemical weapons treaty. Will any na-tion . . . take seriously our recent efforts to negotiate a stricter regime controlling these weapons? I think not. A U.S. decision to go ahead with binary weapons will send the opposite signal.[38]

Soviet Incentives for CW Arms Control

To evaluate these conflicting arguments about the impact of the binary program on CW negotiations, it is necessary to try to understand possible Soviet incentives for accepting an agree-ment requiring them to give up their formidable CW stocks.

The primary military incentive for a mutual CW ban would be to eliminate the U.S. CW threat. But the Soviets would probably enter into such a ban only if they believed that the United States possessed a credible CW retaliatory capability. Faced with such a U.S. capability, the perceived military advantages of the USSR's initiating the use of CWs would be substantially neutralized because a credible threat of CW retaliation forces the attacker to wear cumbersome protective gear and to operate with detection, decontamina-tion, and other specialized equipment that can seriously de-grade his combat performance. Estimates of such degrada-tion range from 30 to 60 percent.[39]

Another way to reduce the perceived value to the Soviets of retaining their CW arsenal is for the United States to possess adequate protective equipment and other defense capabilities of its own. If the Soviets recognize that U.S. forces can operate reasonably well in a chemically contaminated environment – or at least that the performance degradation is roughly symmetrical – they will see less military advantage in the use of CW.

The bilateral CW military equation is not the only possible source of Moscow's interest in a CW ban. The Soviets, who have supported nuclear nonproliferation as staunchly as the United States, presumably also have a strong interest in curbing the proliferation of chemical weapons and in assuring themselves in a verifiable way that such potential adversaries as China do not pose a serious CW threat. Politically, the Soviets have long portrayed themselves in international forums as champions of the abolition of chemical arms and would regard a leading Soviet role in achieving such a result as adding to their international standing. Reinforcing this motivation is the desire to remove the stigma attached to the USSR as a result of widely publicized reports in recent years of the use of chemical weapons by the Soviet Union and its allies.

Existing U.S. Retaliatory Capabilities

Of these various factors affecting Soviet incentives to join a CW ban, Soviet perceptions of U.S. CW retaliatory capabilities are most directly affected by the prospect of binary weapons. But to assess the impact of binaries, it is necessary first to try to understand how the Soviets evaluate current U.S. CW capabilities. Of course, this is a difficult task, and the difficulty is underlined by the wide disagreement that exists among U.S. evaluations of current U.S. capabilities.

There is agreement both that total U.S. stocks of CW agents produced between 1940 and 1969 are large and that the militarily usable portion of those stocks is relatively small. Two-thirds of all those stocks are stored in bulk containers, and neither the munitions nor the munitions-filling capacity exists to make this bulk agent militarily serviceable. Moreover, two-thirds of the remainder is filled with munitions for which delivery systems no longer exist. Thus it is widely agreed that only about 11 percent of U.S. CW stocks are militarily useful.[40]

The dispute is over the adequacy of this 11 percent as a deterrent. Critics of binaries argue that existing CW retaliatory capabilities are sufficient, emphasizing those categories of munitions, such as 155 mm artillery shells, in which the United States is currently in relatively good shape. The administration and its supporters point out the sizable deficiencies, including the lack of sufficient quantities to conduct sustained CW operations, the absence of CW munitions for carrying out particular missions (especially "deep strike" operations behind enemy lines), and the problem of the deterioration of the CW stockpile (including the munitions and agent) over time.

In any event, it is widely recognized that the quantity and quality of militarily useful U.S. stocks constitute the more pessimistic side of the current U.S. CW picture. But there is another side as well. Since 1975, prompted in part by an appreciation of the CW-readiness of Soviet military equipment captured in the 1973 Middle East war, there has been a resurgence in efforts to strengthen U.S. CW combat capabilities. Although most public attention has focused on congressional disapproval of requests for the binary program, the overall chemical warfare budget since 1975 has increased at a higher rate than the Department of Defense (DOD) budget as a whole.

Of the $1.1 billion requested by DOD for the FY 1985 Chemical Warfare Preparedness Program, only funds requested for the binary program (less than 10 percent) were deleted by the Congress. The lion's share of CW appropriations has been devoted to such mundane activities as introducing more realistic and rigorous chemical warfare training for U.S. troops, integrating chemical warfare planning more effectively into U.S. combat doctrine, purchasing modern protective suits and decontamination equipment, demilitarizing obsolete and unsafe munitions, upgrading the serviceability of existing munitions, and instituting organizational changes such as assigning CW specialists to more army units and creating new units specializing in chemical decontamination and reconnaissance.[41]

In assessing U.S. chemical warfare capabilities, the Soviets, with their traditional emphasis on the operational dimension of warfare, may well place as much importance on such elements as training, doctrine, and organization as they do on the quantity and quality of the U.S. CW stockpile. Indeed, despite the highly visible floundering of the binary program, the Soviets may conclude that U.S. chemical warfighting capabilities are incrementally improving rather than wasting away.

The Impact of Binaries

How would the binary program affect Soviet perceptions of U.S. retaliatory capabilities? To address this question, it is important to understand that binaries essentially provide a newer, safer way of packaging and delivering existing types of nerve agents. Binary munitions consist of two relatively nontoxic chemical substances that mix and become highly lethal only when the munitions are in flight toward their targets. Thus, they offer certain advantages over "unitary" weapons in safety of handling, storage, and transport, which contribute to their utility in combat situations. Moreover, new binary munitions could increase the variety of combat missions that could be performed with CW such as the use of aircraft-delivered Bigeye CW bombs in a deep-strike role. And given the ceiling that the absence of munitions and munition-filling capacity effectively places on the quantity of serviceable unitary weapons, the production of binaries could enable the United States to increase the size of its CW arsenal, or at least prevent it from shrinking over time through deterioration.

Naturally, it is hard to tell how the Soviets evaluate the

prospective addition of binary capability. On the one hand, because binaries are basically a modern means of delivering the existing generation of nerve agent, they will not require the Soviets to change their approach to protection, decontamination, or detection drastically. Moreover, the Soviets are aware that, to be effective, chemical weapons have to be located in the theater of military operations, either stored there permanently or deployed forward in a crisis. Given the questionable attitude of allied governments toward prepositioning additional CW on their territory and the extensive lift capacity that might be absorbed in deploying binary CW forward in a crisis, the Soviets may well discount the extent to which new binary munitions would add quantitatively to U.S. stocks actually usable in combat. In addition, the Soviets may figure that, even with the greater storage safety of binaries, neither U.S. allies nor U.S. congressional districts where CW are stored will want to see a major increase in the size of chemical stocks and that this—combined with congressional resistance to spending money on CW—will effectively cap the U.S. CW threat.

On the other hand, production of binaries would make clear to the Soviets that, in the absence of arms control, the United States will remain in the CW business indefinitely. Any hopes they might have had that the U.S. deterrent capability would wither away over time would disappear. The binary program would also open up new CW combat options for the United States, such as use of cruise missiles armed with CW, that the Soviets would presumably prefer to keep closed. And in terms of the quantitative threat, new binary production would ensure that, at a minimum, serviceable U.S. munitions would not decrease and—depending on the volatility of budgetary pressures, allied reactions, and domestic public opinion—might even substantially increase.

On balance, the Soviets probably believe that the binary program would involve a significant but incremental improvement in U.S. CW retaliatory capabilities. Would it prompt them to take major offsetting steps, stimulate a new U.S.-Soviet CW "arms race," or foreclose opportunities for arms control? Presumably not. Would they feel challenged or threatened by it in the same way, for example, that they might feel challenged by U.S. advanced ballistic missile defense capabilities? Not at all. Would it increase Soviet incentives to achieve an effective mutual ban on chemical weapons? Almost certainly yes — although to a limited extent.

But saying that the production of U.S. binary weapons would probably increase Soviet incentives for CW arms control is not the same as saying that going forward with binaries would be *sufficient* to ensure the negotiation of an effectively verifiable agreement. Nor is it the same as saying that binaries are even necessary to reach such an agreement. To evaluate whether an active, congressionally funded U.S. binary program would be necessary or sufficient to promote successful negotiations, it is important to consider why agreement has so far not been achieved. Is it because the Soviets have not judged existing U.S. CW retaliatory capabilities sufficient to warrant giving up their military advantage in CW? Or is it because the Soviets have been unwilling — for a variety of doctrinal, historical, bureaucratic, and other reasons — to agree with Western requirements for verifying an agreement? Or are both explanations responsible?

Current Impasse in CW Negotiations

International discussions on banning chemical weapons have been underway in multilateral arms control forums since the 1960s. Not much progress was made, however, until an intensive series of bilateral talks in the late 1970s resulted in agreement on most issues dealing with the scope of the treaty and even on certain aspects of verification. Nonetheless, critical differences remained on verification — with the United States pressing for rigorous measures, including on-site inspection to monitor several of the treaty's provisions, and the Soviet Union strenuously resisting such measures. With bilateral talks suspended since the end of the Carter administration, CW arms control has largely been pursued at the multilateral Committee on Disarmament in recent years.

These multilateral talks have produced some progress, including the tabling of a U.S. draft treaty as well as some significant, if glacial, Soviet movement on the inspection problem.

Despite this progress, the negotiators remain far apart on verification. The question may be raised, however, whether verification is the only, or even the most fundamental, obstacle to agreement. In this connection, it has been suggested that the Soviets, rhetoric notwithstanding, have not really been willing to give up their CW stockpiles as long as the United States has been unprepared to take action to bolster the credibility of U.S. CW capabilities. Instead, the USSR has been waiting the United States out, watching its domestic debate carefully, and using a tough Soviet position on verification as a throttle to hold off agreement. It might also be argued that Soviet interest in a CW ban has declined over the last 20 years as Soviet investment in CW capabilities has continued and perhaps grown. If this general view of Soviet behavior is correct, then an active U.S. binary program could have a positive impact on the negotiations if the program were seen by the Soviets as substantially neutralizing the military advantages of their CW stocks.

On the other hand, it might be argued that the Soviets have found existing U.S. CW capabilities – combined with the nonproliferation and other political benefits of a CW agreement – to be a sufficient inducement for them to accept a mutual CW ban. According to this alternative view, the absence of congressional approval for the binary program has not been a significant factor in Soviet behavior. Agreement has not been reached because of differing views on verification, not because the existing U.S. CW capabilities have not given the Soviets sufficient incentives to abandon their own stocks. Some support for this argument is provided by Soviet willingness on a number of occasions to make concessions in the absence of any realistic prospect of congressional funding for the binary program, such as their acceptance in February 1984 of the concept of continuous on-site inspections to monitor the destruction of CW stocks. If the Soviets had wanted to block agreement as long as the fate of the binary program remained uncertain, it seems doubtful that they would have come as far as they have in the negotiations.

We cannot at this time be certain, of course, which of these views is correct—whether the Soviets are currently prepared to trade away their CW stocks in exchange for the elimination of existing U.S. capabilities (if the United States would only relax its position on verification) or whether they will seek to perpetuate the impasse while they wait to see if the United States will let its deterrent erode. But we should recognize that, whether or not the Soviet position on verification is also being used by Soviet negotiators to conceal a reluctance to get rid of CW, it constitutes a serious obstacle to agreement in its own right. Moscow's approach to CW verification reflects a powerful Soviet antipathy to intrusive verification measures, an antipathy based on a long-standing tradition of state secrecy and supported by influential bureaucratic protectors, particularly in the internal security apparatus and the military.

Indeed, the Soviet attitude toward verification constitutes an obstacle to a CW agreement that is virtually independent of Soviet perceptions of the momentum of U.S. CW modernization programs. The funding of U.S. binary production might or might not have a significant impact on the willingness of the Soviets to give up their CW capability; it would have little relevance at all to their negotiating position on verification. It would be one thing if U.S. CW capabilities constituted a potentially grave challenge to Soviet security—such as, for example, a proven, effective U.S. ballistic missile defense. In such a case, the Soviets might be under great pressure to make major negotiating compromises, on military capabilities as well as on verification principles. But U.S. CW capabilities—with or without binaries—constitute no such threat. The Soviets may see some benefits, both political and military, in concluding a CW agreement. But they certainly don't "need" one. They see little pressing reason to sacrifice what they consider to be important principles of sovereignty and security in order to accept U.S. proposals on verification.

This is not to suggest that the Soviets will never budge on verification and that it will consequently be impossible to arrive at an agreement that the West regards as effectively verifiable. But if the Soviets are prepared to alter their position eventually—enough to make such an agreement possible—it will be because of such factors as a Soviet desire to improve bilateral relations, an East-West political climate that permits somewhat greater openness in the Soviet Union, and a Kremlin leadership able to overcome traditional internal resistance to intrusive verification measures—not because the U.S. Congress has finally funded the binary program.

Binaries and the Prospects for CW Arms Control

Thus it is not clear if the U.S. binary program is necessary to promote successful CW arms control negotiations. The binary program could be expected to add to Soviet military incentives to give up their own CW capabilities, and it would probably not do much to stimulate offsetting Soviet efforts or foreclose arms control negotiating options. But the real question is whether existing U.S. capabilities, together with some other political and military incentives, already provide the Soviets sufficient motivation to part with their CW arsenal—and that question we are simply not able to answer.

An easier question is whether support for the binary program would be sufficient to produce a satisfactory agreement, and the answer is it would not. The positive impact it would have on Soviet perceptions of U.S. CW capabilities would not be translated into greater flexibility on critical verification issues. That greater flexibility—if it is to materialize at all—will depend on different incentives.

The sensible conclusion seems to be that one's views about the advisability of binary CW production should not be based on the impact the program may have on the negotiating process. That impact is just too difficult to assess. The decision on binaries should be made on the basis of the merits of the program itself—its implications for deterrence, its technical effectiveness, and its impact on proliferation.

The MX Debate

The uniquely gruesome qualities of nerve agents make the debate on binary CW munitions a particularly emotional legislative confrontation. But the defense controversy in recent years that has received the most public attention and that has involved the highest strategic stakes has been the debate over the MX ICBM. Moreover, the MX debate provides a good example of how arguments about the negotiating value of weapon systems can get out of hand and begin to dominate much more important considerations.

The MX Program

The MX, if and when it becomes operational, will not set any speed records for U.S. weapon procurement programs. The decision to proceed with development of a new land-based missile experimental was taken by President Nixon in the early 1970s, although initial planning goes back even further. Designed as a follow-on to the U.S. first-generation MIRVed ICBM, the three-warhead Minuteman III, the MX was intended to serve two key strategic objectives.

First, it would give the United States the capability to destroy hardened military targets such as ICBM silos and would thus make available to U.S. strategic planners a wider and more flexible range of targeting options, as advocated by Secretary of Defense James R. Schlesinger in 1974 and supported by succeeding U.S. administrations. In this regard, it was seen as a means of offsetting the large asymmetry in hard-target-capable systems that the Soviets were expected to achieve with the deployment of their large MIRVed ICBMs – the SS-17, SS-18, and SS-19. With this counterforce mission in mind, the new missile was designed to have the maximum throw-weight permitted under the SALT regime and to carry 10 highly accurate and powerful warheads.

The second principal strategic objective the MX was supposed to serve was ICBM survivability. Concerned by the rapidly improving accuracies of Soviet MIRVed ICBMs and aware that the 1,000 Minuteman and 54 Titan ICBM silos would grow increasingly vulnerable to a Soviet first-strike, U.S. planners were determined to deploy the new missiles in a way that would permit the bulk of them to survive such an attack. But reconciling the requirement for survivable basing with the requirement for a missile large enough to house 10 powerful warheads proved to be a formidable technical and political challenge.

Four administrations, a handful of blue-ribbon panels, and thousands of experts in and out of government spent countless hours trying to solve this problem. The solution chosen by the Carter administration was the "racetrack" or multiple protective shelter system, under which 200 MX would be shuttled deceptively among 4,600 shelters so that the Soviets could not fix the precise locations of the 200 missiles. After discarding the Carter plan to some degree in response to pressures from politicians in states where the racetracks would be based, the Reagan administration first turned to a stopgap scheme of placing the MX—now down to 100 missiles—in existing fixed silos while continuing to explore several more survivable basing possibilities for the longer term. When that approach met stiff congressional opposition, further study was conducted and a new concept emerged—closely spaced basing or "dense pack." According to the concept, closely spaced MX silos would be adequately survivable both because of the substantially increased hardness of the planned silos and because incoming Soviet warheads would tend to destroy one another in accordance with a technical phenomenon labeled "fratricide." Notwithstanding whatever technical merit the plan may have had, it was, in the words of one senior official, "counterintuitive" and never commanded much public or congressional support.

It was left to the President's Commission on Strategic Forces—or the Scowcroft Commission as it was called after its chairman, former NSC adviser Brent Scowcroft—to find a way out. They did by proposing a politically elegant compromise: deploy 100 admittedly vulnerable MX in fixed silos, develop a new small, single-warhead ICBM to ensure future survivability, and promote arms control arrangements that encourage movement toward such stabilizing un-MIRVed systems. One of the Commission's underlying rationales was that, given the survivability of U.S. strategic forces taken as a whole, it was permissible to deploy 100 vulnerable missiles as long as steps were taken to ensure future survivability, especially the development of the single-warhead Midgetman.

Buoyed by bipartisan support for the Commission's recommendations, the MX passed several legislative tests. In fiscal year 1984, $4.1 billion was authorized for producing the first 21 missiles. In the spring of 1984, however, with the Soviets having walked out of INF and refusing to schedule a resumption of START, the MX ran into trouble. The Defense Department's request for $5 billion to produce another 40 missiles was cut to 15 missiles in the House and 21 in the Senate. The final compromise version of the fiscal year 1985 bill required four affirmative votes in the spring of 1985, two in each house, to fund additional missiles beyond the original 21.

The most controversial feature of the administration's MX plan was the basing of the missiles in vulnerable fixed silos. Having been told over and over again about the dangers of Minuteman vulnerability and the importance of going ahead with a more survivable MX, the legislators were reluctant to approve a program that, in the view of many of them, would have a destabilizing strategic impact. A vulnerable MX, the opponents argued, would give the Soviets incentives to strike first in a crisis. They said it was preferable to wait for the more survivable, less destabilizing Midgetman.

Proponents countered that, as the Scowcroft Commission had pointed out, the United States was in no immediate danger of overall strategic vulnerability and could therefore afford, as a transitional measure, to deploy the MX in fixed silos as it proceeded at a responsible pace with Midgetman. The MX was needed to counter the Soviets' now-major advantage in hard-target capability and to support the U.S. doctrine of more flexible targeting options endorsed by four successive administrations. As a practical matter, the proponents argued, the MX was available right away; the alternatives were down the road.

Arguments Over the MX's Negotiating Value

In all budget battles where the stakes are high and the votes are close, advocates on each side reach for every half-way plausible argument that can conceivably bolster their case. Therefore, it was to be expected, especially with the hiatus in nuclear arms control negotiations, that the 1984 MX debate would conspicuously feature arguments about the impact of MX on prospects for reviving the talks and getting them on a more productive track. But it was perhaps surprising the extent to which debate over the value of the MX as a negotiating tool tended to overshadow the debate over its value as a contribution to the U.S. deterrent. The terms "bargaining chip" and "negotiating leverage" became virtually household words. And as the battle got more intense, the claims of both sides tended more and more to become caricatures of negotiating reality.

Thus, many opponents of the MX began to argue that the MX was demonstrably not a good negotiating tool because the Soviets had broken off the negotiations even though the Congress had earlier supported the missile. But the fact that the Soviets broke off the talks hardly shows that they have no incentive to limit the MX (or the D-5, or ALCMs, or any other U.S. systems). It simply shows that, in the short term, they placed a higher value on doing what they felt they had to do in response to initial U.S. INF deployments than on continuing their efforts to limit U.S. strategic capabilities, which they knew could be resumed at any time of their choosing.

Arguments by MX supporters contained their share of distortions as well. They asserted, for example, that congressional support for MX was necessary to get the Soviets back to the negotiating table and that failure to support the MX would persuade the Soviets that they could achieve their objectives without negotiations or sacrifice. But these arguments essentially assume that Soviet strategic arms control objectives are confined to curbing the MX – and that the D-5, ALCMs, and the other U.S. offensive arms programs (not to mention the Strategic Defense Initiative [SDI]) give the Soviets little reason to negotiate. Moreover, these arguments also exaggerate the degree to which the Soviet decision to reconvene arms control talks will depend on the fate of particular U.S. weapon programs like MX rather than on Soviet attitudes toward improving bilateral relations, the Kremlin succession struggle, and a wide range of other considerations.

Although the negotiating value of the MX has gotten more attention than it deserves, the impact of a major weapons program on prospects for arms control is, after all, a valid area of inquiry. But that impact should be examined with greater care and objectivity than is possible in the highly polarized atmosphere of an impending defense budget vote.

Bargaining Chips vs. Negotiating Levers

In public discussions of the negotiating value of the MX, attention often turns to whether the MX is a "bargaining chip." The discussion then becomes confused as observers cite what they consider to be contradictory statements by administration officials. On the one hand, the administration asserts that the MX provides leverage in the negotiations and will make the Soviets more receptive to the limits proposed by the United States. On the other hand, the administration states that the MX is not a bargaining chip (that is, not a trading asset to be bartered with) but rather a strategically vital weapon system that the United States fully plans to deploy. But if the administration has no intention of trading away all or any of its planned MXs, the observer asks, how can the MX provide negotiating leverage?

The statements are not contradictory. Even if a weapon system is not bartered away (fully or even partially), its deployment may influence the other side's negotiating behavior by altering the value the other side places on its own systems, making them more or less expendable in negotiations. It could be argued that, even if the MX were fully deployed, its ability to destroy Soviet silo-based ICBMs would provide negotiating leverage by inducing the Soviets to accept reductions in their newly-vulnerable systems. Thus, the MX could be a negotiating lever without being a bargaining chip.

Indeed, this is precisely the sense in which the Scowcroft Commission considered the MX to be a valuable source of U.S. negotiating leverage. Abandoning the MX, the Commission's report pointed out rather obliquely, would "undermine the incentives to the Soviets to change the nature of their ICBM force."[42] General Scowcroft put the matter somewhat more clearly in testimony on the Hill. The MX, he said, would "convince them [the Soviets] that their big missiles in silos are wasting assets."[43] Thus, according to this view, the MX would decrease Soviet incentives to hold on to their large, MIRVed ICBMs, including their "heavy" SS-18 ICBM, and make them more amenable to U.S. proposals for substantial cuts in those systems.

It is true, as discussed in an earlier chapter, that U.S. hard-target-capable systems can and probably will induce the Soviets to decrease the share of their ICBMs deployed in fixed, vulnerable silos and to move to greater reliance on lighter, more survivable systems that are inherently less destabilizing. It is questionable, however, whether the MX is specifically needed to promote this evolution.

Indeed, the evolution is already underway. The Soviets have already flight-tested two new solid-fueled ICBMs (the single-warhead SS-X-25 and the MIRVed SS-X-24), both of which may be deployed in mobile launchers as well as in silos. Early development work on the MX over a decade ago may well have been responsible for encouraging the Soviets to move in the direction of these new mobile systems, and in that sense the MX may already have exerted some leverage on Soviet planning. But the actual deployment of the MX does not now seem essential to persuade the Soviets to keep moving in that direction.

To the extent that the Soviets need further encouragement, it will be provided by the D-5 SLBM, which will also be hard-target-capable, which will be deployed in much greater numbers (and only three years later) than the MX and which the Soviets probably figure will remain safe from congressionally imposed cutbacks. It will also be provided by Midgetman, which of course is still only on the drawing boards but is also planned to have the capability to destroy hard targets and has so far enjoyed an extended honeymoon with both liberals and conservatives on the Hill. And if further encouragement is needed, it can be provided by the U.S. ALCM force (which can destroy hard targets although not as promptly as ballistic missiles) and even by our Minuteman IIIs (whose probability of destroying silos is much lower than that of the MX or D-5 but cannot be ignored by the Soviets).

Moreover, although the Soviets can be expected – with or without prodding by the MX – to decrease their relative dependence on fixed ICBMs, they will not necessarily be induced to abandon or even reduce substantially their 308 SS-18s, their largest, most destructive ICBMs. The United States must assume that the USSR (like the United States) will retain a substantial number (i.e., more than 308) of vulnerable, silo-based ICBMs in their force because such systems offer a variety of technical and economic advantages over mobiles, for example in ease of command and control, higher alert rates, and lower operating costs. Whether the Soviets choose to retain 308 or many fewer SS-18s among their silo-based ICBMs will depend on many factors, including the perceived military utility of the SS-18s compared to that of lighter, newer, more efficient Soviet ICBMs; costs; bureaucratic considerations, such as pressures from the various missile design bureaus; and the provisions of future arms control agreements (i.e., the levels of various ceilings and subceilings). Vulnerability will encourage – indeed is already encouraging – an overall move to greater survivability of the Soviet strategic forces. It will not determine the composition of the silo-based force that is retained, however.

If vulnerability will not necessarily guarantee a reduction in SS-18s per se, might it nonetheless be expected to make the Soviets more receptive to the U.S. START proposal's overall intention of reducing the most destabilizing components of Soviet strategic forces – ICBM warheads and throw-weight? The answer is mixed. A determination by the Soviets to make a greater share of their land-based forces survivable does not necessarily imply reductions in the total number of ICBMs (because some fixed ICBMs could simply be replaced by mobiles on a one-for-one basis). Nor does it necessarily mean a reduction in MIRVed ICBMs from the SALT II level of 820 (because some fixed MIRVed missiles could similarly be replaced by mobile MIRVs).

In practice, however, vulnerability is likely to increase receptivity to reductions – at least from the SALT II levels. Mobile MIRVed ICBMs (if the Soviets indeed make their SS-X-24 mobile) might be expected, for reasons of practicality, to be lighter than the fixed missiles they replace, and this could result in a reduction in ICBM throw-weight. And moving to mobiles is likely to involve an increase in operating costs as well as a variety of technical and operational complications that might give the Soviets grounds for replacing fixed systems with mobiles on less than a one-for-one basis, thereby achieving a net decrease in missile numbers.

It is interesting, in this connection, that the Soviet START proposal reportedly calls for a cut in MIRVed ICBMs from the SALT II level of 820 to 680, and it seems reasonable to assume that the growing vulnerability of Soviet fixed, MIRVed ICBMs contributed to Soviet willingness to take this positive step.

The MX as a Bargaining Chip

In assessing the MX as a negotiating instrument, it is also important to look at its potential value in the traditional role of a bargaining chip – as a negotiating asset that could be bartered away, fully or partially, for suitable Soviet concessions. In some respects, Soviet incentives to negotiate a cutback of U.S. MX deployments are not very great. For reasons discussed earlier, including their plans to deploy mobile ICBMs, the Soviets are not overly concerned by the MX and have not sought in their own START proposal to place special constraints on it. Moreover, having followed the domestic difficulties encountered by the MX, the Soviets will be hesitant to pay a premium price for a system whose chances of survival in Congress are uncertain at best. Even if the MX manages to survive, the number of missiles to be deployed—plans call for 100—will not be very impressive when measured against typical Soviet missile production runs. In this connection, it is worth recalling that the Soviets in March 1977 turned down a U.S. proposal involving an offer to forgo a planned deployment of 200 MX.

Nonetheless, the trading value of the MX should not be dismissed too readily. When and if it is deployed in 1986, it could well be the most capable missile ever fielded by either side—with a probability of destroying hardened targets perhaps exceeding that of the much larger SS-18. Although the Soviets know that the D-5 and probably Midgetman will also have hard-target capabilities, they may well see a fixed-based system under continuous, reliable command and control as more threatening (especially in terms of first-use) than other U.S. systems.

As far as political survivability is concerned, the MX may have been on the ropes recently, but prudent Soviet planners are presumably not ready to count it out. They have witnessed even more remarkable resuscitations of U.S. weapon programs, including the B-1 and even the MX itself (by the Scowcroft Commission in 1983). On numbers, the currently programmed deployment of 100 missiles (with 1,000 warheads) may seem paltry by Soviet standards and does not by itself constitute a first-strike threat to Soviet fixed assets. But the Soviets must take the MX's potential war-fighting capabilities seriously—both for limited attacks and, when combined with D-5 and Pershings, for a first strike. Furthermore, the Soviets might not assume that 100 is a permanent

ceiling. With the House and Senate conferring on how much
to cut back and slow down MX deployments, the idea of going above 100 may now seem laughable. But the Soviets may
give some credence to the veiled warning contained in the
Scowcroft Commission's report:

> A large deployment of several hundred MX missiles
> should be unnecessary for the limited but very impor-
> tant purposes set forth above. Should the Soviets refuse
> to engage in stabilizing arms control and engage instead
> in major new deployments, reconsideration of this and
> other conclusions would be necessary.[44]

So what would the Soviets be prepared to trade for this
somewhat tarnished but basically sturdy delivery vehicle?
In SALT II, the Soviets proposed a ban on new types of
MIRVed ICBMs, which would have precluded the MX and
their SS-X-24. The United States rejected the proposal. Would
the Soviets still be interested in an MX for SS-X-24 deal?
Probably not. When the Soviets made their offer, the MX
program looked a lot healthier than it does today (Soviet
worst-case assumptions about the future notwithstanding),
and the SS-X-24 was still several years from flight-testing.
Now that the new solid-fueled missile—which can help solve
Soviet vulnerability problems at the same time it boosts their
warhead totals—has been successfully tested, the likelihood
of stopping it must be considered small. A more plausible
deal would be to ban any additional new type of MIRVed
ICBM. This would prevent the Soviets, for example, from
deploying a solid-fueled replacement for the SS-19, which
would be heavier and more threatening than the SS-X-24.

It is possible that, in addition to this ICBM modernization constraint, we could obtain some reductions in existing
Soviet ICBMs in exchange for an offer to forgo the MX. But
the reductions would probably be modest and would presumably be undertaken at a rate that permitted the Soviets to
get most of the useful life out of the missiles they were retir-
ing. Thus, if the Soviets decided (probably for reasons hav-

ing little to do with arms control) that they were prepared to phase down or phase out their SS-18 force, they might agree to take down a substantial number (perhaps 100–150) of their SS-18s if the United States agreed to cancel the MX. Much of course would depend on questions that are impossible now to answer regarding the situation prevailing at the time such an offer was made. For instance, would the MX outlook be clearer by then, one way or the other? Would developments in Soviet forces change the bargaining equation?

MX and Negotiations

An active MX program is not an indispensable requirement for negotiating a START agreement that serves U.S. interests. At the same time, it is not the failed and worthless bargaining chip that many of its opponents, citing the Soviet walkout, claim it to be. It has value as a negotiating asset, but public debate so far has tended to obscure the nature of its value.

It is not necessary as a lever to pry the Soviets away from their reliance on large, fixed, MIRVed ICBMs. The Soviets can be expected to move in that positive direction with or without the MX—indeed, with or without arms control. But the MX does provide negotiating capital that can obtain some useful concessions from the Soviets. Of course, with the MX now trading at a discount in view of its domestic problems, those concessions would not be earthshaking. The United States cannot, for example, expect to swap the MX for the entire SS-18 force. But it probably could obtain limitations or reductions that would by no means be trivial.

The catch, of course, is that the United States would have to give up the MX—altogether or some number of them. And that raises the key question of the intrinsic merits of the weapon system. Would an MX deployment strengthen deterrence or undermine stability? What is the strategic value of the particular capabilities that the MX has to offer? Should the United States wait for the Midgetman or proceed with a fully developed, available system? These are the kinds of considerations that should dominate our internal debate. Questions regarding the negotiating value of the missile have a legitimate role to play in the debate, but those questions can only be addressed in a speculative manner and, in any event, are of secondary importance.

6

Some Conclusions and Policy Implications

Misconceptions and slogans have so far dominated the public debate on negotiating leverage. The key assumptions on which both sides have based their arguments are misleading in important respects.

On one side of the debate there has been the assumption that competitive arms acquisition and arms control are fundamentally incompatible. According to this view, U.S. actions in the field of weapons development stimulate Soviet reactions — and in this surging ahead and catching up, arms control gets shunted aside. In other words, if one party is negotiating from strength, the other must be negotiating from weakness, and because neither side will bargain from a position of disadvantage, meaningful bargaining will be precluded. Restraint, these advocates maintain, is more likely to result in agreements than competition.

But the record of the past 15 years demonstrates that arms competition and arms control are not incompatible. Indeed, it demonstrates that U.S. defense programs are essential to persuade the Soviets to accept significant constraints on their military capabilities. To be sure, the record points out that, in some important instances such as the introduction of MIRVs, moving ahead with weapon programs beyond a critical threshold in the procurement cycle can rule out arms control options that might be promising. Usually in such cases a qualitative balance is upset irreversibly and the other side feels it has no choice but to take offsetting steps. What this suggests is that, in certain cases, if arms control is to be pursued productively, it must be pursued before such thresholds are crossed. It does not mean that defense programs are incompatible with or unnecessary for arms control — for even in such cases, the initiation of a credible U.S. program is what stimulates Soviet interest in mutual limitations, even if self-restraint proves necessary at a certain stage to keep that interest alive.

In many other cases, there will be less risk of precluding arms control by proceeding with U.S. defense programs. In INF, for example, the U.S. deployments in Western Europe are reversible and do not foreclose any negotiating options. In a variety of other cases, U.S. programs do not upset qualitative or quantitative balances and do not produce much in the way of competitive Soviet reactions. For example, binary CW, unless produced in huge quantities, would not be expected to have much impact on Soviet CW programs. And although critics have argued that the MX would stimulate the development of a corresponding Soviet missile, the Soviets' new, 10-warhead SS-X-24 appears to be a logical progression in their ICBM program that would have been pursued regardless of the MX. Whatever else can be said about the negotiating value of binary CW and the MX, neither can credibly be accused of provoking arms races or precluding arms control.

Just as it is misleading to argue that competitive arms acquisition and arms control are incompatible, it is also wrong to assume — as it often is at the other pole of the debate — that active U.S. defense programs can virtually guarantee productive negotiations. Momentum in U.S. weapon programs, while a necessary condition for success, is clearly not enough. The ability of the United States to exert leverage over Moscow's negotiating behavior is both limited and hard to predict.

First, there is a tendency to overestimate Soviet interest in limiting U.S. programs through arms control. Although the Soviets may be prepared to pay a considerable price to head off some new U.S. developments, other developments they are content to deal with through their unilateral defense efforts. And given their comparative advantage in deploying large numbers of systems, they have not been under much pressure to negotiate limits on the size of U.S. programs.

Second, the Soviets place a far higher priority on unilaterally obtaining and preserving the capabilities they consider necessary to meet their security requirements than on limiting U.S. programs of concern to them through arms control. Certain Soviet capabilities such as the hard-target ICBMs needed to threaten U.S. strategic forces have, for all intents and purposes, been off-limits to arms control. Indeed, U.S. weapon programs will have a greater impact on Soviet force structure over the long run by inducing the Soviets to alter their force requirements than they will have in the short run by providing incentives for them to trade away systems they consider essential for meeting existing force requirements.

Third, like the Soviets, although to a lesser extent, the United States often prefers to protect its own capabilities rather than limit the Soviet Union's. By withholding certain U.S. programs, partially or fully, from the bargaining process, the United States reduces Soviet incentives to make concessions and increases the difficulties of achieving its negotiating objectives. This is not to suggest that it would be desirable to put all U.S. potential bargaining assets on the negotiating table. Clearly, overall U.S. interests are often better served by proceeding with U.S. defense plans even if doing so means forfeiting useful negotiating leverage. But the fact that the United States often chooses to forgo the use of available leverage provides one reason why impressive momentum in defense programs does not necessarily translate into an ability to influence Soviet behavior. Indeed, the reluctance of both Washington and Moscow to allow negotiations to cut into their defense muscle helps explain why arms control has so far had such a marginal effect on both sides' force structures.

Fourth, nonmilitary considerations play a key role in the process, diluting the impact of strictly military incentives and making Soviet behavior less predictable. Factors that we may barely be conscious of, such as a power struggle in the Kremlin, may have a decisive effect on prospects for agreement.

In a most fundamental sense, U.S. negotiating leverage is limited because the Soviet Union has the resources and the will to compete with the United States in the absence of arms control. The Soviets will sign an agreement only if, at a minimum, it leaves them no worse off than they would be without it. It is tempting to think that, with its much stronger economic and technological base, the United States could force the Soviets to choose between accepting U.S. proposals or engaging in an all-out arms race that would be a painful and losing proposition for them. But given the realities of its democratic system, the United States is not in a position to threaten such a contest with any credibility. And at the level of effort the United States could plausibly sustain, the Soviets would be able to keep up. After all, arms racing is what the centrally planned, military-oriented Soviet system does best.

In describing the relationship between U.S. defense programs and Soviet negotiating behavior, the term "leverage" is therefore a misleading one. Leverage implies not only the ability to exert coercive influence but also an ability to exercise that influence in a mechanistic, predictable way. U.S. defense programs, as robust as they are or could foreseeably be, give the United States neither of these capabilities.

Some Implications for U.S. Policy

It is useful to consider what these observations may imply for U.S. policy, particularly for the U.S. approach to weapons procurement and arms control.

Weapons Procurement

The fundamental lesson for arms procurement is to plan, without reference to arms control, to acquire the weapon systems that the United States believes are necessary to meet U.S. military requirements—neither cutting back those plans in anticipation of a successful outcome to negotiations nor padding them with systems assumed to provide additional negotiating leverage.

If the United States bases its force plans on assumptions about the likely results of negotiations, it will find itself dependent on achieving those results. And because it is not prepared—in terms of force planning—for a failure to achieve agreement, it will be in an even less advantageous position to obtain the results on which it had become dependent. Instead, it should seek forces that would be sufficient in the absence of agreement and then propose arms control measures that, by constraining Soviet capabilities, would enable the United States to cut back its planned deployments and meet its military objectives at lower cost and perhaps also with greater security.

If the United States acquires weapon systems for their presumed negotiating value, it will end up distorting its force structure without necessarily strengthening its bargaining position. There are several reasons why "bargaining chips"—used here in the narrow sense of weapons purchased primarily for negotiating purposes—are not a good investment.

Weapon programs that do not serve U.S. security objectives well are not very valuable as negotiating assets. Lacking intrinsic merit militarily, they will not command strong support at home and accordingly will not have much credibility at the bargaining table. In addition, given the inherent difficulties in knowing how the Soviets perceive various U.S. military capabilities (for example, how they perceive current U.S. CW capabilities and how binary munitions would affect that perception), it is a chancy business to acquire forces in the expectation that they will have a decisive impact on negotiations. If the United States buys systems strictly for their assumed bargaining value and then fails, for whatever reasons, to achieve agreement, it would be stuck with weapons it really did not need. Bargaining chips, moreover, are a luxury the country cannot afford; they displace forces that could better meet U.S. security needs.

Hanging on to weapons long after they should have been retired in the hope of trading them away for something of greater value makes as little sense as purchasing new bargaining chips. Just as the United States should not pay the Soviets very much to get rid of the few hundred remaining obsolescent SS-4 intermediate range-missiles, the Soviets will be reluctant to trade their front-line systems for U.S. dinosaurs. It is in this light that we should view decisions by recent administrations to retire from the operational inventory 10 Polaris submarines that were growing old and costly to maintain, to phase out the old, liquid-fueled Titan ICBMs that had become a more serious hazard to Americans than Russians, and to withdraw 1,000 obsolete nuclear weapons from NATO's stockpile as a gesture to Western public opinion in connection with the decision to deploy Pershings and GLCMs. None of these sensible acts of "unilateral disarmament" was included in arms control negotiations because it was correctly understood that none had very much trading value and all served U.S. interests, such as costs, safety, and public opinion, whether or not the Soviets reciprocated.

Now that the legislative and executive branches have gotten into the habit of debating the negotiating value of U.S. programs, it is unlikely that weapon systems will be judged exclusively on the basis of their contribution to U.S. security. But it is important that such negotiating considerations not dominate the debate. Programs that do not have a persuasive security rationale and can only be sold on the basis of bargaining-chip arguments may not be very good at strengthening either U.S. security or U.S. negotiating positions. On the other hand, programs that serve U.S. security requirements are likely to provide the strongest negotiating incentives.

Approach to Arms Control

If arms control is to play a significant role in promoting U.S. security interests, it is important that Washington understand both the value and the limitations of U.S. defense programs as tools of negotiation. Washington needs, for example, to try to gain an appreciation of the priorities the Soviets place on limiting various U.S. programs and to make the most of those cases where the Soviets are especially interested in constraints and the United States is prepared to accept such constraints. Recognizing that the Soviets have generally been most concerned about new and challenging U.S. technological developments, the United States has on some previous occasions sought to trade off Soviet interest in stopping such developments for a U.S. interest in limiting existing or prospective Soviet capabilities. Thus, in SALT I, the United States linked the conclusion of the ABM Treaty, which dealt with Soviet concerns about the impending U.S. missile defense capability, with the conclusion of the Interim Agreement, which addressed U.S. concerns about the Soviet buildup in offensive forces. Similarly, in SALT II, the United States traded a finite-duration moratorium on SLCM and GLCM deployment and certain constraints on ALCMs for modest limits on Soviet ICBM capabilities.

In the future, the United States should look for trade-offs that could maximize its available leverage. One possible trade-off that has occurred to many observers is to link the Soviet goal of constraining U.S. space weapon programs to the U.S. goal of reducing Soviet ICBM capabilities. The Soviets appear genuinely concerned about the prospect of an effective U.S. defensive shield and could be expected to pay a price to block the Reagan SDI before it gains too much momentum. But even assuming the United States were prepared to give up future space weapons options—and the Reagan administration has so far demonstrated little inclination to do so—it is not clear how high a price Moscow would pay, especially in the next few years. The Soviets recognize that the possibility of an effective U.S. nationwide defense is at least a decade or two away and that much could happen between now and initial deployment. The necessary technologies may not pan out. Or at some stage a new administration could take office and eliminate the program. The Soviets may calculate that they could afford to wait until the U.S. program is terminated unilaterally.

So, although the Soviets would probably be willing to make some cuts in offensive forces to stop the SDI, even in the near term, those cuts might well be more modest than the United States would consider commensurate with its abandonment of a potentially significant technological edge. This is not to discourage efforts to trade off areas of U.S. and Soviet comparative advantage—only to suggest that such deals may often be quite complicated (especially when an unproven future technology is pitted against a valued existing capability) and not as advantageous as one might expect.

The United States should also make the most of Soviet political incentives for agreement, not just technological ones. For example, it might be argued that, in view of the strong foreign policy motives the Soviets had for concluding SALT I, the United States might have held out for a somewhat better deal. Of course, assessing Soviet nonmilitary incentives is a very speculative business. But the United States has tended in the past to give too much emphasis to "hardware" incentives and should make a greater effort to understand factors that often exert a greater influence on Soviet behavior.

Just as the United States should make the most of available opportunities, it should also be conscious of occasions in which continuing U.S. programs beyond some point of no return may preclude opportunities to exploit available leverage. Of course, not all activities in the weapons acquisition and deployment cycle are irreversible. The deployment of U.S. Pershing IIs and GLCMs in Western Europe, for example, is reversible and does not preclude any INF negotiating options. But some activities are irreversible, such as MIRV flight-testing. Although deferring MIRV flight-testing in 1968 may not have led to a MIRV ban, proceeding with

MIRV tests certainly made a subsequent prohibition a long shot, as the Soviets felt compelled to match the knowledge and capability irreversibly gained by the United States through its tests. Often it will be in the overall U.S. interest to continue with its programs beyond a point of no return despite the missed negotiating opportunities. But it is essential that it make such choices with as clear an appreciation of their implications as possible. The United States should recognize, for example, that proceeding with the flight-testing of its F-15-based ASAT interceptor system beyond some number of successful tests involves some risk of narrowing certain ASAT arms control possibilities.

Finally, it is important to approach arms control negotiations with a realistic understanding of the limits of available U.S. negotiating leverage. The current momentum in U.S. strategic modernization programs has undoubtedly gotten the Soviets' attention and given them tangible reasons to accept negotiated constraints on their strategic capabilities. But it is necessary to recognize, in evaluating what constraints are achievable with the help of stepped up U.S. programs, that the Soviets have not been resting on their oars. The momentum they generated in the late 1960s, which had such a dramatic impact on key measures of strategic capability in the 1970s, has continued into the 1980s. They probably do not see the U.S. forcing the pace of the strategic offensive arms competition to a degree that would strain their capacity or will to cope in the absence of agreement.

This does not mean that, from the standpoint of military incentives, the Soviets will refuse to cut a deal. They have made proposals in START that improve marginally on SALT II. This readiness to improve on SALT II can be attributed in part to changes in the Soviet force structure, such as reducing reliance on fixed ICBMs, that were encouraged by increasing U.S. hard-target capabilities. Moreover, the likelihood that Moscow will be engaged in substantial force restructuring over the next decade opens up the possibility that they could go beyond the marginal improvements already proposed. But they will do so only if they believe both sides are making roughly equal sacrifices. And, despite U.S. arguments that the U.S. START proposal would stabilize the strategic balance and serve the interests of both sides, the Soviets claim that it is one-sided and would place them at a disadvantage. They will therefore resist the ambitious cuts in ballistic missile capabilities the United States has proposed, especially in the absence of what the Soviets consider to be sufficient cutbacks in planned bomber and cruise missile levels.

There is nothing wrong with setting ambitious goals in arms control or making opening proposals that give negotiating room. But if U.S. objectives and the leverage the United States has to achieve them are not roughly in balance, it will face certain risks. Inflated public expectations may arise, which, if not fulfilled, could result in strong criticism of the negotiating effort or pressures for unwarranted concessions. Indeed, the failure to meet expectations could have a disruptive effect on U.S. weapon programs, as critics of the administration's arms control policy seek to hold those programs hostage to progress in negotiations. Any administration may decide, for tactical or substantive reasons, to stake out a tough negotiating position and thereby accept such risks. It may believe, for instance, that an agreement on less advantageous terms would not meet minimal U.S. requirements. But if it is to accept such risks, it should at least be fully aware of what is involved – and that requires a realistic assessment of negotiating incentives.

Supporters of negotiating from strength are correct in asserting that a strong U.S. deterrent and active U.S. defense programs are essential if the United States is to have any prospect of achieving militarily significant arms control agreements with the Soviet Union. But success in negotiations requires more than these military incentives. Among other things, it requires the sort of bilateral relationship that provides political incentives for accommodation. It requires a balance of bureaucratic forces and other domestic pressures (in both the Soviet Union and United States) that permits a productive process of bargaining to take place. It

requires that the United States set sound, realistic negotiating objectives that meet U.S. requirements while taking
Soviet interests into account. It requires firmness, skill, and
persistence in pursuing those objectives, combined with a reasonable amount of flexibility in devising specific approaches
that can achieve them. And above all, it requires the willingness of both the Soviet Union and the United States to
accept equitable constraints on their military programs in
the interest of achieving agreements that can strengthen
their mutual security.

Notes

1. Somewhat clouding the ABM example was the precipitous decline in congressional support for Safeguard after its initial legislative victories. By August 1971, the Senate Armed Services Committee was only willing to authorize the deployment of two sites and advanced preparations for two more (out of the original 12-site plan).

What incentive, it might be asked, did the Soviets have to complete the negotiations when their primary concern – an effective, nationwide U.S. defense – seemed politically unattainable? Why not let the talks fail and proceed with their own program? A plausible answer is that they understood that, if they took advantage of an absence of treaty limitations by moving toward an effective nationwide defense, public resistance to a similar U.S. system would almost surely collapse, and they would again be confronted with an arms race they were unlikely to win. Thus, it was the initial, congressionally supported commitment to a U.S. ABM program (and its successful series of flight tests in 1969) that most affected Soviet negotiating behavior, not the subsequent decline in the program's support. Also, although Soviet acceptance of severe limits on ABM deployment was probably motivated primarily by concern about the implications of a potentially superior U.S. system, U.S. arguments about the destabilizing impact of nationwide missile defenses may well have had an impact on Soviet decision making.

2. Secretary of Defense Harold Brown testified before the Senate Foreign Relations Committee in 1979 that the Soviets had been expected to deploy at least 100 more MIRVed ICBMs than permitted by the 820 sublimit, and that the SS-18 ICBM was capable of carrying 20 or even 30 warheads, compared to its ceiling of 10.

3. There is wide disagreement on why SALT I did not result in a MIRV ban. Some maintain that, if we had persisted, the Soviets would have agreed to a ban on the testing, production, and deployment of MIRVs, which would have conceded to the United States an advantage in testing experience but not a right to produce or deploy. The problem, in this view, was that the Nixon administration, unwilling to override military opposition or take on conservative critics, was not truly determined to ban MIRVs. Others argue that, once the United States achieved a demonstrable edge in MIRV technology through its test programs, the Soviets were simply not willing to permit the United States to retain that edge through a ban on testing, even if they could be sure the United States would not clandestinely deploy its tested capability. And still others hold that, even if the United States had not begun MIRV flight-testing in 1968, the Soviets would not have been interested in a MIRV ban because of the potential advantages in MIRVing that their large throw-weight boosters gave them.

4. In cases such as the BW Convention and the ABM Treaty protocol, in which the Soviets agreed to give up options of relatively minor military importance, the compensating benefits they hoped to achieve were not primarily of a military character. (The role of nonmilitary incentives is discussed in chapter 4.)

There have been continuing doubts that the Soviets have lived up to their obligation to destroy BW stocks. The Sverdlovsk anthrax epidemic of 1979, thought by many to be the result of an accidental explosion at a facility where BW were clandestinely stored, has fed such doubts. Illegal Soviet retention of BW would disqualify the BW Convention as an example of Soviet willingness to give up military capabilities without receiving military quids pro quo.

5. The Soviets can, of course, pose a threat to U.S. territory with cruise missiles of similar ranges, but their lack of forward basing tends to limit that threat. They can deploy ALCMs on intercontinental-range "heavy" bombers, but without forward bases, they cannot strike the United States with ALCMs deployed on

shorter-range aircraft. They can deploy SLCMs on submarines patrolling off U.S. coasts, but without forward port facilities, the long transit times make this an inefficient (not to mention vulnerable in view of U.S. antisubmarine warfare capabilities) approach to deployment. In terms of GLCMs, the Soviets have no politically feasible land-basing opportunities within range of U.S. territory for cruise missiles of less than intercontinental range.

6. Soviet persistence in constraining cruise missiles has been strongest in the case of long-range SLCMs and GLCMs, where the Soviets have never deviated, either in SALT or START, from their position that the deployment of such systems should be banned. Their attitude toward ALCMs has been less strict. Both in SALT and START, the Soviets abandoned initial attempts to ban long-range ALCMs and agreed instead to permit them within certain limits. But these concessions were acceptable only because the potentially open-ended character of the U.S. ALCM threat would be bounded significantly by other provisions, especially a ban on deploying long-range ALCMs other than on heavy bombers (thus foreclosing a U.S. option to deploy them on forward-based aircraft) and the inclusion of heavy bombers equipped for ALCMs in the sublimit on multiple-weapon delivery vehicles (thus limiting the number of platforms on which ALCMs could be deployed).

7. The Soviets have argued that minimal warning time – and thus the risk of a surprise first strike – is a concern to them with respect to the GLCMs as well as to the Pershings. They maintain that, while short time of flight is responsible for the Pershing II providing minimal warning, the GLCM is designed to evade detection altogether and may, despite its much slower speed and longer flight time, actually provide less warning than the Pershing.

8. Of course, advanced technological developments and counterforce capabilities are not mutually exclusive categories. There is considerable overlap; for example, guidance systems capable of providing hard-target-kill accuracies may well involve advanced technologies. Nonetheless, the achievement of U.S. and Soviet hard-target ballistic missile capabilities has been an evolutionary process involving incremental improvements from generation to generation. At least for the purposes of this analysis, this incremental process can be distinguished from the acquisition, through major technological advances, of qualitatively new systems and capabilities, such as ABM, ASAT, and cruise missile systems.

9. The Soviets considered several of the elements of the March

1977 proposal objectionable and one-sided. In addition to the reduced limits on heavy ICBMs and MIRVed ICBMs, the ban on further ICBM modernization would have halted their fourth-generation ICBM modernization programs far short of plans. The Soviets also objected to the public handling of the proposal as well as to its radical departure from the Vladivostok framework. Nonetheless, if the Soviets had placed much importance on heading off U.S. ICBM counterforce capabilities, they might have been expected to make a counterproposal more favorable to them that contained a ban on the MX.

10. U.S. Department of Defense, *Soviet Military Power, 1984* (Washington, D. C.: GPO, 1984), 24.

11. Although heavy bombers equipped for ALCMs were included in the SALT II limit of 1,320 multiple-weapon delivery vehicles, they were the least restricted of the three types of systems included in that category. MIRVed ICBMs were restricted by a subceiling of 820, and MIRVed SLBMs by a subceiling of 1,200, but each side was given the right (which neither would obviously want to exercise) to use the full quota of 1,320 for bombers carrying ALCMs. Moreover, although MIRVed ICBMs could carry a maximum of 10 warheads and MIRVed SLBMs a maximum of 14, heavy bombers equipped for ALCMs could carry an average of 28 such missiles per aircraft. Thus, the maximum number of ALCMs theoretically attainable under SALT II was much greater than the maximum number of ballistic missile warheads that each side could possibly attain. Similar provisions of the Soviet START proposal would allow either side, if it cared to do so, to devote its entire allotment of strategic weapons to ALCMs.

12. With the SS-17, SS-18, and SS-19 carrying 4, 10, and 6 warheads respectively, and the U.S. Minuteman III (then and still the only deployed MIRVed U.S. ICBM) carrying only 3, the Soviets were able to overtake the United States in ICBM warheads very soon after they began deploying MIRVed versions of their fourth-generation ICBMs. But the United States began MIRVing its SLBMs (with 10-warhead C-3 and later 8-warhead C-4 missiles) much earlier than the Soviets, and the resulting lead in SLBM warheads enabled the United States for several years to more than compensate for the Soviet lead in ICBM warheads. The U.S. lead was narrowed and then eliminated, however, as the Soviets deployed first their MIRVed ICBMs and then their MIRVed SLBMs (the 7-warhead SS-N-18 and the SS-N-20 with 6-9 warheads).

Currently, although the USSR has a higher share of its missile warheads on ICBMs and the United States has a higher share on SLBMs, each is moving toward the SALT II ceiling of 1,200 MIRVed ballistic missiles. And because of its large advantage in ICBM fractionation (i.e., warheads per missile) and its rough equivalence in SLBM fractionation, the Soviets will be able to deploy more warheads on their roughly 1,200 ballistic missiles than the United States will. It is currently not clear whether the Soviet lead in ballistic missile warheads will grow large enough to overtake the traditional U.S. lead in bomber weapons and thus give the Soviets an overall numerical edge in strategic weapons.

13. The U.S. 1970 "comprehensive" proposal called for a limit of 1,710 ballistic missile (ICBM and SLBM) launchers, which was the number deployed by the United States, as well as a ceiling of 250 on launchers of modern, heavy ICBMs like the Soviet SS-9. (The United States had none.) At that time the Soviets had 1,560 operational ballistic missile launchers and 400 more under construction, as well as 222 operational SS-9s and 60 under construction.

14. The Soviets had pressed to conclude the ABM Treaty separately and to deal with offensive systems later. Recognizing that the principal military incentive for the Soviets in SALT I was to constrain the U.S. ABM program, the U.S. administration believed such a sequence would squander U.S. leverage needed to achieve limits on Soviet offensive systems, particularly the SS-9. They therefore successfully held out for concluding the two agreements concurrently and claimed this linkage was responsible for the limits on Soviet offensive forces. It should be noted that not all observers support this explanation. Some believe that the outcome on offensive forces was possible because the United States permitted the Soviets to do virtually everything they planned to do and that just about the same result could have been obtained if the United States had agreed to the Soviet proposal to conclude the two agreements sequentially.

15. These reduction figures assume a ceiling of 2,000 delivery vehicles and the SALT II data base figures of 2,283 U.S. and 2,504 Soviet systems. Most of the U.S. reductions would have been taken in "mothballed" (i.e., nonoperational) B-52 bombers, while Soviet reductions would have come from operational but aging Bison bombers, single-warhead SS-11 ICBMs, and single-warhead SLBMs.

16. The Soviets, according to Secretary of Defense Harold

Brown in SALT II testimony, were planning to deploy more than 920 MIRVed ICBMs. The United States had not decided what mix of MIRVed Minuteman III ICBMs, MIRVed MX ICBMs, and MIRVed SLBMs would have been deployed under the Vladivostok ceiling of 1,320 MIRVed ballistic missiles (later reduced to 1,200). The maximum number of MIRVed ICBMs the United States could have deployed was 750 (550 Minuteman IIIs and 200 MX), in which case the proposed sublimit would have required a reduction of 200 from the planned level. But it is likely that the preferred MIRV mix would have called for fewer than 750 MIRVed ICBMs, in which case the reduction would have been lower – and the discrepancy between U.S. and Soviet reductions under the 550 sublimit much greater.

17. The Warsaw Pact participants claimed that they had 805 thousand ground force personnel, and 987,300 total ground and air force personnel. NATO estimated that the Warsaw Pact force levels were, respectively, 962 thousand and 1,162,000. These figures are presented in John G. Keliher, *The Negotiations on Mutual and Balanced Force Reductions: The Search for Arms Control in Central Europe* (New York, N.Y.: Pergamon Press, 1980), 123.

18. "The Soviet Approach to Arms Control" in *Challenges for U.S. National Security: Final Report of the Carnegie Panel on U.S. Security and the Future of Arms Control* (Washington, D.C.: Carnegie Endowment for International Peace, 1983), 4.

19. Sayre Stevens, "The Soviet BMD Program" in Ashton B. Carter and David N. Schwartz, eds., *Ballistic Missile Defense* (Washington D.C.: The Brookings Institution, 1984), 201.

20. The U.S. March 1977 proposal in SALT II, in which the United States offered to abandon its plans to acquire 200 MX and to freeze further modernization of its ICBM force in exchange for substantial cuts in Soviet MIRVed ICBM capabilities, is perhaps the best example.

21. Robert Legvold, "Strategic 'Doctrine' and SALT: Soviet and American Views," *Survival* 21, no. 1 (January/February 1979), 11.

22. From the U.S. perspective, Soviet movement to smaller systems could be desirable even if those new systems were more effective than the larger missiles they replaced. Smaller systems are more likely to be deployed in a survivable basing arrangement, and this would create less pressure for the Soviets to "use or lose"

their weapons in a crisis. In addition, if arms control constraints on fractionation (i.e., warheads per missile) were to terminate, a larger throw-weight missile would enable the Soviets to expand their number of warheads more than would a smaller missile.

23. As discussed in chapter 5, obtaining this negotiating leverage does not necessarily depend on acquiring a particular type of counterforce system (e.g., the MX) but rather on acquiring a sizable U.S. hard-target capability regardless of the precise mix of U.S. counterforce systems.

24. Benjamin S. Lambeth, "The Political Potential of Soviet Equivalence," *International Security* 4, no. 2 (Fall 1979), 30.

25. Henry A. Kissinger, *White House Years* (Boston, Mass.: Little, Brown and Company, 1979), 821.

26. John Newhouse, *Cold Dawn*, (New York, N.Y.: Holt, Rinehart and Winston, 1973), 235.

27. Speech to Regional Foreign Policy Conference, Birmingham, Alabama. March 22, 1984.

28. David Fewtrell, *The Soviet Economic Crisis: Prospects for the Military and the Consumer*, Adelphi Papers Number 186 (London: The International Institute for Strategic Studies, 1983), 9, 14.

29. Ibid., 8.

30. Ibid., 27.

31. Seweryn Bialer, "A Wounded Russian Bear is Dangerous," *Washington Post*, January 22, 1984, p. C2.

32. Fewtrell, *Soviet Economic Crisis*, 32.

33. Henry A. Kissinger, *Years of Upheaval* (Boston, Mass.: Little, Brown and Company, 1982), 1026.

34. *New York Times*, January 25, 1984.

35. Henry Kissinger, *The White House Years*, 821.

36. The only funds ever approved by Congress for the binary program, which the army has been promoting since 1969, were $3.15 million in FY 1981 that had not been requested by the Carter administration and $20 million in President Reagan's FY 1981 supplemental request. These funds went toward the construction of a building in Pine Bluff, Arkansas, where binary production would take place. But no funds have been provided for production equipment or production itself.

37. Letter to Congressman William Dickinson dated May 16, 1984. U.S. Congress, House, *Congressional Record*, 98th Cong., 2nd sess., May 17, 1984, H4101.

38. U.S. Congress, House, *Congressional Record*, 98th Cong.,

2nd sess., May 17, 1984, H4110.

39. Brad Roberts, "U.S. Chemical Warfare Preparedness Program," Issue Brief Number IB82125 (Washington, D.C.: Congressional Research Service, December 1982), 7.

40. Ibid., 10–12.

41. Ibid., 5–9.

42. *Report of the President's Commission on Strategic Forces* (Washington, D.C.: GPO, April 1983).

43. U.S. Congress, Senate Committee on Appropriations, *S. Con. Res. 26, A Resolution to Approve Funding for the MX Missile*, 98th Cong., 1st. sess., May 1983, p. 95.

44. Report of the President's Commission.